COLLABORATIVE
LEADERSHIP
FOR THE CLASSROOM

COLLABORATIVE LEADERSHIP FOR THE CLASSROOM

Leading Gen Z Children

DON BROADWELL

Collaborative Leadership for the Classroom
Copyright © 2019 by Don Broadwell. All rights reserved.

No part of this publication may be reproduced, stored in a retrieval system or transmitted in any way by any means, electronic, mechanical, photocopy, recording or otherwise without the prior permission of the author except as provided by USA copyright law.

The opinions expressed by the author are not necessarily those of URLink Print and Media.

1603 Capitol Ave., Suite 310 Cheyenne, Wyoming USA 82001
1-888-980-6523 | admin@urlinkpublishing.com

URLink Print and Media is committed to excellence in the publishing industry.

Book design copyright © 2019 by URLink Print and Media. All rights reserved.

Published in the United States of America

ISBN 978-1-64367-673-9 (Paperback)
ISBN 978-1-64367-672-2 (Digital)

15.10.19

To the five million US teachers who, despite the furor going on around their profession, close their classroom door and begin the task of preparing children for their uniquely interactive future.

A special dedication to Major General O.K. Steele (ret) and to the memory of Dr. Thomas Gordon of Gordon Training International.

CONTENTS

Preface 9
Introduction 15

Chapter 1: Changing Leadership: A Brief History 19
Chapter 2: Basic Collaboration 34
Chapter 3: Advanced Collaboration 52
Chapter 4: Situational Leadership Revisited 72
Chapter 5: Millenial Children and No Child
 Left Behind 92

Epilogue 109
References 113
Appendix 1 119
Appendix 2 121
Appendix 3 123
About the Author 125

PREFACE

Following graduate school and seven years in the Marines, I lived for forty years among educators. By the fall of 2011, I was pleasantly retired, playing golf on occasion, not expecting to conduct another leadership training or sit at a keyboard to write. For keeping busy, for pocket change, and for the company of young people, I delivered pizza on the weekends.

One day, on a whim, I googled "Collaboration/Obama," and came across a *USA Today* article "Obama Bets on Collaboration." That got my attention. Beginning in 1982, I had taught collaborative leadership to classroom teachers for the better part of two decades, withdrawing from that field in 2002 when standardized testing began to dominate of the curriculum.

While teaching weekend workshops at Seattle Pacific University, I had kept my nine-to-five job supplying library books to Pacific Northwest schools. This placed me in the position of absorbing the ever-present criticism of education while also having the trust of librarians, who willingly shared their dismay. As a book rep, I have been education's proverbial fly in the wall, listening and watching as everyone from the US Congress to the Gates Foundation seemed to know more about teaching than the professionals who performed it. I had been intrigued when, in the 1990s, under the rubric of "decentralized decision-making," collaboration was tried and found wanting. Could a return to collaborative deciding be at hand?

My interest grew the further I searched. At length, I discovered President Obama's initiative on collaboration, the Open Innovation Portal, and its half-a-billion program for promising new ideas. After years of arguing for children's voices in classroom decision-making, I had found the invitation I sought. In 2011, After a decade-long thrust toward standardized tests, the teacher/student relationship would finally come back to the spotlight. . . . or so I thought.

During the Human Potential days of the 1990s, participative leading, as educators called it, was in vogue. But participation proved to be amorphous, time-consuming, and unproductive. By 2000, to no one's surprise, school administrators began to stomp their feet. Top-down leading returned in force. Command and control once more became the accepted modality, at least in practice. Participative decision-making continued to get lip service. But given the time needed for group deliberations and the confusion over method – not to mention the lack of accountability – the collapse of "participation" could have been foreseen. In any event, the time had come for me to dip my toe back in the water. I rebooted my nonprofit Collaborative Center and once more commenced to teach.

In general, leadership has undergone more than a few changes since the early days of civilization. Certainly, the Industrial Revolution called for a rational model, and this was provided by Frederick Taylor's Principles of Scientific Management, first published in 1911. Taylor, however, overlooked much that the ancients had to offer. Some 500 years before Christ, Lao Tzu wrote, "A leader is best when people barely know he exists." We know much about what the leader *is*. He is tall, male, well groomed, well dressed; he is deliberate in his actions and circumspect in thought. But what does a leader *do*? The leader solves problems. He does more than drive people with alpha male demands (the transactional model), more than inviting workers to share in the mission and goals (the transformational model). Leaders do more than meet the needs of employees (Greenleaf's servant leader model). Despite being conceived by Dr. Thomas Gordon in 1974, the collaborative model is new and innovative. Time will tell if there is room for Gordon's model in our nation's schools, or as I argue below, there is merit to a combination of models, one that proves facile, productive, spontaneous, and even beguiling for children and teacher alike.

My first exposure to leadership theory came some 50 years ago at the behest of the U.S. Marine Corps. Following three months of Officer Candidate School and six months command training, I got my first assignment to lead a platoon at Camp Pendleton, California. Following eighteen months of infantry duty, I was moved to the USMC Mountain Warfare Training Center in California's High Sierras. There, along with twelve other guides, I was tasked to train marines in the science of over-snow combat and, during the summer, in the practice of cliff assault. The marines we trained each month would not form a fighting unit in and of themselves. They were expected to serve as advisors to large-scale operations should warfare break out at high elevations, which it has. . . just not in 1965.

After 30 months in the mountains, I bounced between desk jobs, then took my leave to study theology. My seminary training gave me my first exposure to group decision-making, and I have not looked back. I have watched as group-process leading (as it was called in the 1960s) morph into conflict resolution, then into conflict prevention, negotiated leadership, no-lose leading, participatory leading, and now leading via collaboration.

Collaboration is an appropriate description. Today, led by the technology sector, Corporate America is learning ideas can come from any level of the organization. Today, considering the many exhortations to collaborate, all that is missing is how and when. These are topics I address in this book.

I am indebted to Captain (later Major General) Ort Steele for showing me the human side of authority while we were assigned to the Mountain Warfare Center. Among other things, Steele told me to quit insisting the marines salute me. "You never know when you'll need these guys to dig you out from a pile of snow." I took his advice. I remember the times that followed as the closest of team bonding. They were among the happiest and most challenging of my career.

The day I met Steele, he invited me for a run. As we jogged in the crisp mountain air, he plied me with questions about his new job. Who were these guides he'd be working with? What should he expect from us? What did we expect from him? He was quick to assure me I'd have a job as his assistant, and soon placed me in charge of the winter syllabus. Since he was a novice skier, he quickly became my pupil. I was beneath him in rank, and I revered him for naming me his second during the winter phase of training. (Another lieutenant got the well-deserved second-in-command title during the climbing syllabus.) My esteem for Ort Steele has never wavered.

From Captain Steele, I learned never to issue an order I could not expect to enforce. Also, nobody knows how to do the job better than the man who is doing it. *Don't tell people how to do things, instead tell when what you want done and leave them alone.* This advice actually goes to Gen. George Patton, who said, "Never tell people how to do things. Tell them what to do and they will surprise you with their ingenuity." Unlike Patton, who had a reputation for gruffness, Steele carried a gentility that would make *Gone with the Wind's* Rhett Butler proud; during our years together, I never heard him raise his voice.

I will try to emulate Ort Steele as I write. I will not raise my voice. There is nothing in this book that one ought to do to become a more effective teacher. There are no shoulds, no oughts, no musts. There is only invitation. In fact, you will discover you are already more of a leader than you know. Today teachers live in a hypercritical environment, one that robs them of confidence and makes them think there is little room for mistakes. They must control their classroom and have leadership down pat. How do they do this without seeming like Genghis Khan at recess? I will address such riddles in the pages ahead. History shows us leadership changes. Once more, our understanding of leadership is about to change.

INTRODUCTION

I have yet to meet a young person who enjoyed his or her schooling. In hindsight, school was an exercise in compulsive obedience. As is written, *"They must attend school for most of the day and they have only very limited influence on what happens there. They are pressured to learn complex and esoteric subjects like algebra, chemistry, and European history, which rarely have immediate relevance to their day-to-day lives."* (Milner, M., 2015)

As mentioned above, I am retired. My work these days is delivering pizza, mostly because I like being around young people. It keeps me young myself. What has become obvious to me is that most of our young workers got little from their education. After dropping out of high school, most of my young friends completed their high school equivalency (GED); some are even enrolled in local community colleges. Others, ambition intact, are studying vocations like computer science, information technology, industrial drafting, and the like. The youngsters all tell me the same; high school neither challenged them nor set them free. Uniformly, they were eager to get away, to spread their wings and fly.

There are dim signals that schooling is changing. In Washington State, 2015 Teacher of the Year Lyon Terry is being rewarded for allowing his 4th graders more voice than he gives himself. Will Terry set a precedent for others to follow? Can we somehow expand the voices to children to a point where they help determine outcomes in the classroom? What model will teachers adhere to? And what does this have to do with classroom leadership?

My goal is for teachers to share leading with students, to model collaborative leading in situations of choice. *Collaborative Leadership for the Classroom* follows a developmental format, meaning I use a building block scheme to add small units to what has already been learned. Chapter 1 describes the evolution of leadership thought from Lao Tzu, writing prior to the Christian Era, through the 1990s Human Potential Movement to the present Obama-inspired emphasis on collaboration. Chapter 2 describes collaboration under basic conditions—for example, when there is no anger or hidden agenda. Here, full disclosure is in place. It is the best way I know to teach collaboration's fundamentals. Chapter 3 details how to collaborate amid complications like angry feelings and when stakeholders are not forthcoming.

In chapter 4, I examine twin-poled leading, flexible problem-solving that originates along a spectrum. This is the chapter that reconciles Authority and Participation and creates a new understanding of situational leadership. The key ingredient is personal values. The role played by values is spelled out so there is no doubt that authority and collaboration are both valid starting places for leaders; they exist side-by-side. Collaboration becomes one of many problem-solving options, but it can be the option of first refusal, inviting teachers to shift their leader base away from traditional authority (see appendices 2 and 3).

Chapter 5 looks at generational changes that point to collaboration as the optimal style for Gen Z students. I provide case study material from teachers who use my bi-polar design. Chapter 6, the epilogue, explores the political drama unleashed by No Child Left Behind. Former D.C. educational chancellor Michelle Rhee once argued that "The civil rights movement didn't work things out by consensus" (Rhee 2010, para 9.), but for school reform in the twenty first century, I conclude that collaboration is the perfect choice. In fact, collaboration and school reform will one day be synonymous.

Teachers will find it easier to shape their classrooms into a problem-solving whole than to be the "sage on the stage," the omniscient decider. Teachers can energize their classrooms, gain buy-in from students, and implement solutions together with their kids. Leading becomes as stress-free an activity as reading a book or eating lunch. In the process, teachers can raise achievement to levels they, and the public, desire.

Collaborative leadership brings challenges. Teachers who collaborate must adjust the expectations of children, who will not immediately understand that it is for special occasions. It is not meant to dominate the decision-making process. On occasion, these same teachers must explain to succeeding teachers (those who inherit their class for the following school year) why their children are so vocal. Principals need to understand the method to evaluate their staff. Still, teachers who collaborate release the creative energy of their children, gain buy-in from their classrooms, and find implementing decisions easy thanks to the commitment of their students. They also have the satisfaction of preparing children for a future an order-of-magnitude different from the one for which they themselves were prepared.

Like Tom Gordon, I believe the terms leadership and problem-solving are inter-changeable. In this writing, as in Gordon's Teacher Effectiveness Training (1974), the terms are synonymous. This assumption has proven itself time and again over my thirty-plus years of teaching. Still, the evidence is anecdotal and the time left waiting for empirical proof is short. Only those with the courage of their convictions need to read on.

Chapter 1

CHANGING LEADERSHIP: A BRIEF HISTORY

"We now know that along with everything else, leadership changes"

Barbara Kellerman

I remember the moment when, for me, leadership changed forever. As freshly minted youth pastor of a small New Jersey church, I was tasked with organizing my high school fellowship for a Christmas pageant. Although steeped in authority-based deciding, during the months prior to the event, I had taken loose rein with my kids, placing myself in a listening role more than a directive one. But I had longed for a more hands-on opportunity. The notion of thirty six youngsters needing a Hollywood-style director was the perfect chance for me to take charge. I waded in with barrels blazing, giving orders left and right. My kids were confused and upset.

My misadventure ended when the group's president came to me with, "We want you out of here." Years later I would learn ways I could have stayed in character and still met the groups need for direction. For the moment, I was stunned. I was not over the event when a few youngsters came to my home to see if I was okay. Since that day I have learned a many more lessons, *some of which I liked*.

One thing I learned is that leadership has always changed. From its inception in the pre-Christian era to the middle 20th century, its rate of change has been glacial. Over the past 50 years that pace escalated to something quite intense. Today leadership is in a quandary. Training is a 50 billion dollar per year industry (Kellerman, 2012, p. 154) despite bringing us no closer to leadership nirvana than we were previously. "Bottom line; while the leadership industry has been thriving – growing and prospering beyond anyone's early imaginings – leaders by and large are performing poorly, worse in many ways than before" (Kellerman, B., 2012, p. xv). How do we account for this disconnect when, in fact leadership and followership have both evolved over time? Let's start from the beginning.

From the start of recorded history, kings, princes, and clerics ruled the masses -- so much so that by the 17th century, philosopher Thomas Hobbes framed life as "solitary, brutish, poor, nasty, and short" (Kellerman, 2010, p. xix). Still there were leaders concerned with who and how to lead. In the beginning, there were Lao Tzu, Confucius, and Plato. Confucius (551 B.C.) believed that those in authority should behave as gentlemen. Self-educated, without a platform from which to officially teach, he organized groups of disciples and taught them elements of the leadership he embraced.

Confucius was deeply disturbed by the authoritarian condition of his time, dedicating his life to social reform. His *Analects* (teachings), compiled by students after his death, revealed his primary emphasis on sincerity and his commitment to ethical leadership. He advocated that leaders should be older, wiser, better; as close to perfection as possible. He taught, "Those who wished to secure the good of others have already secured their own" (Anderson, P., 1990, p. 52). He believed that government should make its end the happiness of its subjects, not the pleasure of the rulers. Confucius has been called perhaps the most influential teacher in the history of the mankind (Anderson, 1990, p. 50).

Plato (423 B.C.) was a contemporary in focus and in thought, if younger than Confucius by birth. He too believed in the education of leaders and surrounded himself with students at the Academy of Athens, which he founded. He believed that leading was based in wisdom, and that unless philosophers become kings, or kings become philosophers, cities will have no rest from troubles nor, he surmised, will the human race (*Republic* 473c-d). "Confucius's gentleman leader and Plato's philosopher-king have elements in common: they aspire to perfection; they reflect a context that is leader-centric; and they are of a historical moment in which good governance seemed completely to depend on effective, even great leadership" (Kellerman, 2012, p. 7). The notion of the valiant leader did not begin to wane until 1215, when King John of England was forced to sign the Magna Carta, admitting that his authority was not absolute, and his will could not be arbitrarily put to work. This might have been a bench mark in the history of leadership, but the Great Man theory would not fade easily. It would take another 750 years before scholarship would join reality in promoting gender neutral leadership and exploring the prospect of leader and follower laboring together to decide.

Change, in other words, was slow. Although the Magna Carta was a watershed in which the king was compelled to succumb to his followers, this was, after all, the Middle Ages, when royalty ruled on earth and when God, through the Catholic Church, ruled the masses. It is extraordinary then, that the most durable, the most secular, the most pragmatic of leadership treatises was Niccolò Machiavelli's The Prince (1513). Without at least a casual reading of Machiavelli, one easily falls into the common misunderstanding, using the pejorative term 'Machiavellian' to indicate cruelty as a sought-after leader trait.

In fact, Machiavelli was primarily intent on preservation – of his principality, of peace in the domain, and of course, of his power. "As such, he is grounded in the here and now, does not bow to a moral compass, either religious or otherwise, and his loyalty is to himself and his subjects only" (Kellerman, 2012, p. 9). Machiavelli believed his sojourns into cruelty were necessary based on his faith, or lack of it, in the human condition. Followers, to Machiavelli, were "fickle, ungrateful, pretenders and dissemblers, evaders of danger, eager for gain" (Kellerman, 2012, p. 9). This, together with a glut of crises in the Medici reign, made cruelty a viable option. Consequently, the leader should be good, but *able to be not good*. In any event, Machiavelli viewed cruelty as less abhorrent than a leader's mercy, since "too much mercy allows disorders to continue from which come killings or robberies, activities that hurt the whole community" (Kellerman, 2010, p. 35).

Like Machiavelli, Thomas Hobbes, whose *Leviathan* followed The Prince by 100 years, was concerned with how to keep order in a disorderly world. Like Machiavelli, Hobbes thought followers untrustworthy; they were fearful, rapacious, selfish, and dangerous. He too, argued for an authoritarian, even a totalitarian ruler (the Leviathan of his title). Yet unlike Machiavelli, Hobbes turned his attention from those in power to those without. His focus became followers' rights, specifically to a quality life.

For Hobbes, life under medieval rule was, as mentioned, solitary, poor, nasty, brutish and short.* The sea-change he provoked was to make at least one right of ordinary people superior to any right of their king, the right to life. "The change from an orientation by natural duties to an orientation by natural rights finds its most potent expression in the ideas of Hobbes, who put the unconditional right to life at the center of his argument" (Kellerman, 2012, p. 9). For Hobbes, the quid-pro-quo was simple and revealing – followers would grant absolute power to an absolute ruler, who would in turn, provide them with protection, first to secure their right to life and second, to provide them with a life well lived.

Hobbes and Machiavelli seem of a piece; however, Hobbes based his need for an authoritarian ruler on a different premise, his trade-off of power for protection. John Locke (1632), would expand the rights of ordinary people to include the right to liberty and to own property. His was the first 'social contract' in which government claims derive their legitimacy from the consent of the governed. Locke insisted that unless the leader satisfies the led, he may be recalled, if necessary, by force.

---

* The life expectancy for males during Hobbes' era was 43.6 years. (Woodbury, 2014, para. 3)

Leadership from the Eighteenth to Mid-20th Century

Clearly the period leading up to the American Revolution focused on leadership as a function of authority. Following either Hobbes or Locke, one is led to the need for authority, whether for the powerful's sake or for the masses. There followed a period during which that focus remained intact. The question for leaders became, what makes the leader great? For Tolstoy, given his extraordinary faith in the Divine, the answer was that history is predetermined. As such, kings are slaves to history. For Carlyle (1841), history writ large is tantamount to the history of Great Men who have worked here. Moreover, considering also the writings of philosophers Herbert Spencer and William James, none of this work dealt directly with leading. It simply tried to answer the knottiest of leadership questions of the time: does the man make history, or does history make the man? It fell to philosopher John Stuart Mill (1859) to redirect scholarship to the relationship between leader and follower. This he did by expanding on the limitation of power to be suffered by the community, a limitation he calls the *very meaning of liberty*.

Not unlike philosophers of his era, Mill agreed that "to prevent weaker members of a community from being preyed on by innumerable vultures, it was needful to there should be an animal of prey stronger than the rest, commissioned to keep them down" (Mill, J. S., 1859). But as the king of vultures might also prey on the masses, it was necessary to defend against his intrigues. The aim of patriots, therefore, was to limit the king's power.

Mill was not just preaching against abuse of the magistrate's strength, but also against the pressure of social convention (what today we would call PC, or politically correct). He believed there needs to be protection from the tyranny of public opinion -- possibly because he kept a lover for 30 years, marrying her only after her husband died. The romantic collaboration between Harriet Taylor and John Stuart Mill provided Mill with the inspiration to pen one of his greatest essays on liberty, *The Subjugation of Women*, called "an ardent argument for equality between the sexes, and a consequence of her influence" (Kellerman, 2010, p. 73).

Beyond freedom from harm at the magistrates' hand, Mill believed man should be free to form his own opinions, then to act on them without hindrance so long as the risk and peril are his own. "Neither one person, nor any number of persons, is warranted in saying to another human of ripe years, that he shall not do with his life. . . what he chooses to do with it. He is the person most interested in his own well-being: the interest which any other person, except in cases of strong personal attachment, can have in it, is trifling compared with that which he himself has. The most ordinary man or woman has means of knowledge immeasurably surpassing those that can be possessed by anyone else" (Kellerman, 2010, p. 71). (Compare Oliver Wendell Holmes Jr's, "My freedom to swing my arm ends with the other man's nose.")

Mill's writing echoes through our U.S. Constitution and even the songs of Jimi Hendrix. Although he ignored the darker side of the human condition, Mill is on record as "the most vigorous and optimistic defender of the better angels of our nature" (Kellerman, 2010, p. 73).

Following the Middle Ages Karl Marx and Friedrich Engels (1848), concerned themselves with those without power. The two were concerned with the role of followership, particularly in the role of inciting revolution. They are in the tradition of literature as leadership, rather than being actual leaders. (Marx was a sociologist, educated in philosophy and the law; Engels was a merchant committed to overthrowing the German monarchy.) The historical leader, the man who followed the blueprint of Engels and Marx, was Russia's Vladimir Lenin.

Frederick Taylor was a mechanical engineer and a contemporary of Lenin. Taylor believed that workers were motivated by money. He contrived the idea that piecework and strict supervision would raise performance levels during the Industrial Revolution. As such, he invented tools to streamline workers at U.S. Steel, calculating their every move using a stopwatch. By the 1930s, Taylor's reliance on time-and-motion studies fell out of favor (and were outlawed by congress), but his Scientific Steps of Management (1911) was a breakthrough, lending form and substance to what leaders do – solve problems. Taylor's scientific steps -- Identify the problem, Create alternate solutions, Choose one, and Implement– would resurface in the work of Thomas Gordon some 50 years later.

Taylor was a rough-and-tumble authoritarian, sharing his dim view of human nature with Hobbes, Machiavelli and others who came before him. That view was about to change, with consequences for leaders everywhere.

Postwar Changes in the Psychology of Leading

Next in the lineage of leadership are Douglas MacGregor, Thomas Gordon, Roger Fisher and William Ury. Yet the entire thrust of post-World War II leadership pivots around the prewar study of Abraham Maslow leading to his Hierarchy of Human Needs.

Maslow's needs hierarchy is well entrenched in psychological literature and to a sizable extent in management. What is less known is Maslow lived and studied among the Lakota Sioux during a three-month period during the 1930s for the purpose of learning how Native Americans grew into adulthood. From this experience Maslow formulated stages of development that are pursued by individuals, and even civilizations. He published his hierarchy in 1954, in time to profoundly influence the leadership theorists of the ensuing 60 years.

Maslow criticized traditional psychology for its basis in study of the sick (Freud) and/or animals (B.F. Skinner). He insisted that a study of healthy people would create more and better health among individuals and society-at-large. His axiom -- that people had a strong desire to fulfill their potential -- stands as a paradigm shift in the way we look at men and women in the workplace. His is the seminal development in the study of leadership that influenced scholarship (and management) up to and including the present.

Maslow's hierarchy of needs (next page) states that humans are motivated by the pursuit of unmet needs. According to this theory, if fundamental needs are not satisfied, then one will be motivated to satisfy them. Higher needs such as social and esteem needs are not recognized until one satisfies the needs basic to existence (air, water, food, safety). While such pursuit is not linear – individuals move randomly along the needs hierarchy and even reach for multiple successes at the same time. Maslow's model can nevertheless be used to chart advancement in social cultures as well as in mapping individual attainment.

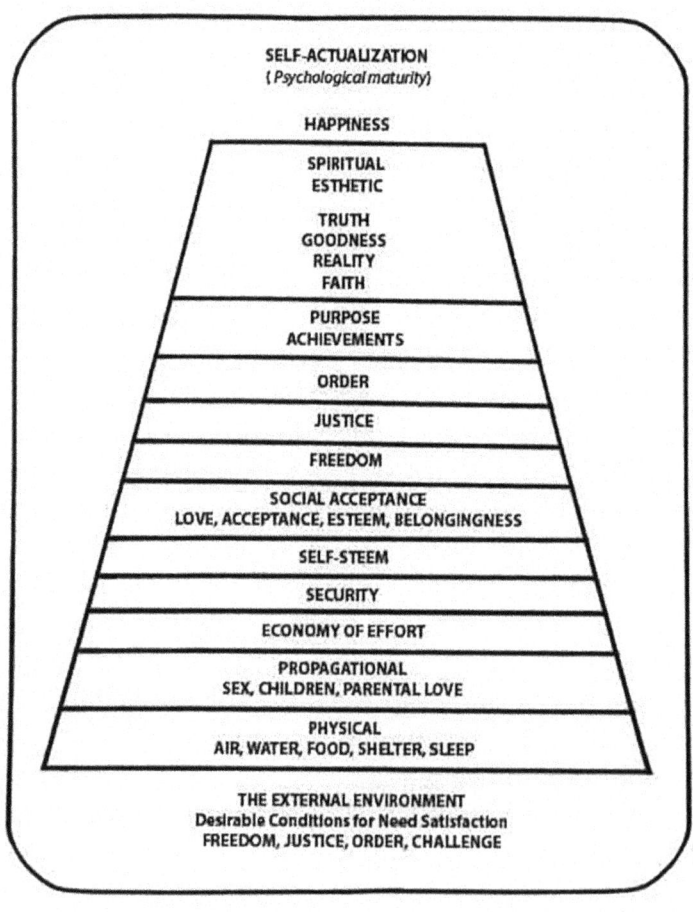

Goble, Frank

My intent here is not to analyze Maslow's pioneering work so much as it is to pinpoint its seldom noted uniqueness. For the most part, Western circles -- North American culture in particular -- have satisfied basic human needs. What intrigues us is Maslow's Meta, or Growth needs, in which social and esteem needs become the primary goal. Note how our schools have prepared young people to achieve their social and esteem needs. Meta needs, meaning friendship, belonging to a group, giving and receiving love, and eventually recognition, attention, social status, accomplishment, and self-respect, are the preeminent needs of our entire society. Those are especially keen among the young. Thanks to teachers, those needs are honored in the classroom, even if misunderstood and under appreciated by education's critics.

An early disciple of Maslow, and the man who gets credit for spoiling the Hobbesian view of human nature, was Douglas MacGregor. MacGregor was in fact, a contemporary of Maslow who conceived the notion that people were not averse to work (the old Theory X*), rather that work can be as natural as play if the conditions are favorable (MacGregor's Theory Y). In *The Human Side of Enterprise* (1960), MacGregor noted people will be self-directed to meet work objectives, will be committed to quality and productivity, but only if rewards are in place that address higher needs. Moreover, most people can handle responsibility because creativity and ingenuity are common in the population. MacGregor makes

---

* Most people find work innately distasteful and they will attempt to avoid it.

the point that a command and control environment is not effective because it relies on lower needs for motivation.

In Western society those needs are mostly satisfied and thus no longer motivate. "In a Top-Down environment, one would expect employees to dislike their work, to avoid responsibility, to have no interest in organizational goals, to resist change, etc., thus creating a self-fulfilling prophecy" (MacGregor, 2015, para. 4). To MacGregor, motivation seemed more likely with his Theory Y model.

Next in line are the men who leveraged Maslow's Hierarchy to create leader models of their own -- Thomas Gordon, Roger Fisher and William Ury. As we will see in the next chapter (Basic Collaboration), Gordon redefined problems so that they reflect the underlying needs of contrasting positions. For example, in a teacher-student problem, both parties might decide in tandem which solution is best for meeting the needs of teacher and student alike. Gordon's book, *Teacher Effectiveness Training* (1974) sold more than two million copies and *Leader Effectiveness Training* (1977) sold eight million copies. More about Tom Gordon in chapter five.

Fisher and Ury, co-founders of the Harvard Negotiation Project, differ from Tom Gordon's work in that they prefer the term 'underlying interests' to Gordon's underlying needs -- understandable since their project is aimed at Corporate America. Where Gordon's efforts targeted interpersonal problems that stifle teamwork and creativity, Fisher and Ury's canvas is the workplace. For example, 1980's negotiations between Simpson Lumber Company and the federal government revealed the following interests. During the confrontation over survival of the Spotted Owl, Simpson needed a hedge of long-range sustainability and the feds needed protection for an endangered species. Together the sides produced the well-known solution that created islands of tree stands, a home for the Spotted Owl. The government found the process so inviting, it offered Simpson a ten-year moratorium on federal oversight of the company's forests.

In another convincing example, Alaskan fishermen had for decades been herded by the Federal Fisheries Department into fishing on designated days, like hunters who find their prey "in season." Halibut fishermen were intensely troubled because when season arrived, they were forced to ply their waters without benefit of reliable weather. On average, five men and women were drowned each year that "Derby Day" was in effect.

Working with their Halibut men, Alaska fishing authorities solved the problem by limiting the season to a given number of days yet allowed the boats to go out at the discretion of the crew. The total purse is now shared by the boats on a pro-rated basis. The new schedule protected the Halibut species while preserving human life. The resulting regulation created high morale among the fleet and made millionaires out of many of its crew.

Together with Tom Gordon, Fisher and Ury are responsible for much that transpired in leadership circles during the 1990s. During that decade, the *transactional leadership* of Machiavelli, Hobbes, and others was replaced by *transformational leadership*, designed to unite leader and follower using decentralized decision making. Transactional leaders pronounce decisions. [One leader who personified transactional leadership was President Harry ("The buck stops here") Truman. Another would be George ("I am the decider") Bush.] Contrariwise, transformational leaders focus their workers on compatibility, creativity, camaraderie, and a goal orientation among their team. Where the transactional leader believes optimal solutions stem from contrasting positions, the transformational leader believes peak solutions originate through a blending of diverse intentions and ideas. One form of transformational leadership is the school mission statement, a product of the 1990s.

    Next in leadership's lineage is the Servant Leadership of Robert Greenleaf. Writing as a contemporary of Thomas Gordon, Greenleaf opined "Servant-leaders focus primarily on the growth and well-being of people and the communities to which they belong. While traditional leadership generally involves the exercise of power by one at the top of the hierarchy, servant leadership upends the pyramid. The servant-leader yields power, puts the needs of others first, and helps people develop and perform as highly as possible" (Greenleaf, 2015, para.5). Well known leadership theorists such as Ken Blanchard, Stephen Covey, and Margaret Wheatley are among those who subscribe to servant leadership. Question: Who meets employer's needs?

    Greenleaf turns the traditional leadership hierarchy on its head -- idealistic on its own and a hard concept to visualize in practice. Nevertheless, in short form, we can say the transactional leader controls power, the transformational leader shares power and the servant leader shuns power altogether. Greenleaf assumes employees whose needs are addressed will graciously labor for their employer's needs at the same time. Unlike Greenleaf, Gordon believed unmet needs of employers and workers are better aired, balanced and satisfied through a collaborative process, mentioned above. Collaborative leading is where we turn next.

Chapter 2

BASIC COLLABORATION

"Where in the world is there someone who can teach our young people how to collaborate?

Hank Rubin

On another level, remember the Age of Empowerment? Of decentralized decision-making? Of the flattened hierarchy? The 1990s were billed as the time when teachers were granted access to school decision-making. By the turn of the century, group meetings, many poorly timed and crudely organized, faced a backlash that resulted in the dismantling of shared decision making and the restoring of Command-and-Control. As the Kappan Magazine noted in 2010, "Teacher collaboration is a prime determinant of school improvement. Unfortunately, though we talk about it a lot, we don't do it as much as we might hope for. We take pride when we see a few random acts of collaboration in our schools, but the *modal* behavior in schools has changed little over the years,... even in schools that claim to have professional learning communities" (Piercey, 2010, p. 55).

As readers might imagine, unlike the amorphous meetings of the 1990s, participatory leading in the 21st century will operate from a more structured framework. Similarly, collaborating will mean more than partnering. Anyone can lead a collaborative, but to lead *collaboratively?* That is a different animal. And what about students? Classroom leading too can be collaborative. Why are not students included when teachers decide?

Collaborative leadership designates a problem-solving sequence. By the Gordon method, it means a six-step arc that closely resembles Taylor's Scientific Steps. But Gordon removes power from the leader and involves followers *equally with superiors* when deciding. Gordon redefines problems in such a way that underlying interests are acknowledged, and in fact, achieved. It is truly a no-lose proposition, and that is the moniker it gained when Thomas Gordon promoted it in Teacher Effectiveness Training -- the *No-Lose* method of leadership (Gordon, 1974, p. 217). Thomas Gordon and the man who influenced him are where we turn next.

A LEGACY OF MENTORS

Collaborative leadership for the classroom was first envisioned by Dr. Thomas Gordon during the second half of the twentieth century. Gordon earned his PhD in psychology following World War Two, having been enamored with Maslow's Hierarchy of Human Needs. It occurred to Gordon that student needs were often obscured by a teacher's fascination with control. Still such needs appeared valid and if expressed openly, could be accepted by the teacher. The trick would be to get teacher and student to reveal their needs, and here the gentle prodding of the psychologist in Gordon shone through.

At the University of Chicago, Gordon wrote his PhD dissertation on adapting to followers' underlying needs when making decisions, calling it

Group Centered Leadership. His work was roundly dismissed. Not to be disabused of the idea, Gordon published his dissertation, Teacher Effectiveness Training, independently. It became an instant hit and remained on the New York Times Best Seller list for more than 30 months.

I met Dr. Gordon vicariously through my reading and through his Effectiveness Institute in Solana Beach, CA. For his efforts at re-defining workplace, classroom and family problems, Gordon received three nominations for the Nobel Prize. His dream of obtaining a Nobel was never granted and he passed away in 2002.

THE GORDON INNOVATION

Gordon believed the presenting problem – the adversarial dilemma as viewed by opposing parties – was seldom the actual problem. The real problem lay hidden among human needs. The conundrum for leaders was to identify those needs and set them in balance. Gordon wrote that leaders would be more effective if they asked, *"How can we meet the needs of students at the same time we meet the needs of the teacher?"* For example, teacher Leanne Aten was having trouble keeping the halls quiet when her fifth graders returned from recess. When she collaborated with her class, she learned that her students needed a few minutes to unwind. Leanne's need was not to disturb the other classrooms, and when she asked, "How can we have both?" her problem disappeared in a slew of children's ideas. "Now I allow them a little time to visit when returning to the room. The conflict no longer exists! My students are quiet in the halls, and they have a few minutes to chat."

This is the Gordon method at work. But because it involves a concrete sequence and not just a single innovation, it invites a closer look.

THE SET-UP

There are two moments when collaborations come to grief, and neither is included among Gordon's steps. One is what I call the Set-Up and the other I call the Cross-Check. The set-up is where the leader gains permission to influence a new and different process. It is designed to gently shut the door on students disrupting or bowing out before the collaboration is complete. Here is Leanne, setting the stage;

"I explained to my class that we have a problem and that I would like to solve it in a way that we would all feel good. I asked the class if this was a good time, and if anyone felt it was not enough time we could reschedule. No one raised their hand. I explained that I had taken a class designed to help solve situations where both sides are happy with the outcome. I asked permission to use this strategy and everybody agreed."

The importance of the set-up cannot be overstated. Without it, the path is open to anyone who wants to deflect or wants to sabotage because of some unstated need. The preamble goes like this:

- Introduce oneself as a facilitator rather than the decider
- State the purpose (so both sides win)
- Ask if the time is good

- Ask if it is enough time
- Ask if the students are willing to try something new
- Begin assessing needs

Again, do not underestimate the importance of each item in this sequence. Teachers might not control the outcome, but they do maintain control of the process. Such modest control is asserted from the start. Teachers should feel the leader's reins within their hands.

GORDON'S SIX-STEP METHOD

The set-up being complete, students are ready for the Gordon process. The steps in order are,

1. Define the problem in terms of the needs of both teacher and students,
2. Brainstorm for solutions
3. Evaluate those ideas
4. Choose the solution
5. Implement
6. Follow-Up on progress.

These steps are explained in further detail, including the Crosscheck, which comes between steps one and two. (The following section assumes collaboration is best learned from the position of third-party facilitator. In the above example, Aten acted as both stakeholder and facilitator, normally a harder way to learn. Here, I think success revolves around the enthusiasm of her class.)

Step one – Defining problems in terms of needs. After a successful set-up, move directly to needs. Listing needs as they are expressed is helpful to stakeholders, as they can then track the Gordon sequence themselves. A whiteboard or legal pad can be employed. Experienced facilitators know that listing needs in a non-judgmental fashion will allow deeper needs to flow to the surface.

Once listed, needs will invariably lend themselves to an *umbrella word or phrase* -- a condensation of several needs into one summarizing desire. Thus, an equation can be drawn so that the stakeholders can readily track the process. On the board, the facilitator can write: *How can we meet the needs of the teacher (A) while also meeting the needs of students (B)?* Moving forward is simply a case of installing the underlying needs. For example, about wearing hats in the classroom, the equation might look like; How can we have students express their individuality while we maintain order in the room? To this problem there are many viable solutions.

[At this juncture, the concern is not with secret needs or angry rebuttal. Chapter 3 studies such advanced cases. The object at this time is to learn the Gordon steps, and to do so as a neutral facilitator. Also, in order to focus on learning the steps, full and honest disclosure of the stakeholders is expected – at least hoped for.]

The cross-check: transitioning Step one to Step two. Before examining solutions, check to make sure both sides are invested in the process. In a real-time collaboration, if a crosscheck is not completed, one or both parties might revert back to blaming the other for the problem. Blame, once allowed, will thrust all efforts into the trash.

Check with stakeholders individually to see if they want to change their side of the equation. If not, feel free to move ahead. Make sure each 'side' understand the needs of the other. To complete the cross-check, ask the tell-all question: *Is it okay for the other party to have the need(s) they expressed?* Failure to complete the crosscheck means the collaboration is at risk. Other than Gordon's redefining the problem, the crosscheck is the most vital part of the process and the reason, if any, for a collaborative endeavor falling through the cracks.

Step two – Searching for solutions. Once the crosscheck is complete, the facilitator can relax to an extent. Ideally, he or she can even accept silly or untenable solutions; laughter opens the mind to new ideas. Apart from the newness of the steps, this should be a stress-free time. Both sides are comfortable with the process, and the facilitator has kept them from opening a figurative door and fleeing. Each party has had the opportunity to disclose individual needs and honor the other person's need(s). By following the guidelines of brainstorming, they will search for solutions together. When one party offers a solution that mainly meets the other person's need, the second person will often offer an idea that reciprocates. That is when the job of the facilitator is, in spirit, done. But not completely.

Step three -- Evaluating solutions. A successful collaboration should begin to crystallize a solution, and often in the interest of time, step #4 – choosing solutions – can immediately follow step #2. If you find it necessary to evaluate ideas one at a time, try using the 'T' design that Benjamin Franklin introduced to chart financial accounts. This method takes longer, but I prefer it in sticky situations. Informal facilitation can come at a later time.

To set up a 'T' chart for solution #1, head the left side with a minus sign and the right side with a plus. Now list limitations on the left and advantages on the right. Next do the same for solution #2, #3 and so on. When completed, a page full of T charts (and evaluations for each one) should result. You might have four advantages on the plus side and only one limitation, however that one disadvantage is a genuine liability to one party. So, you'll need to calibrate that in your outcome rather than simply count the number of advantages and the number of limitations. This method isolates, or flags, bad ideas. It also demonstrates that your stakeholders are working together to solve their problem.

Step four -- Choosing a solution. By this time in a collaboration, the truly satisfying solution will have bubbled to the surface. Often several ideas are acceptable to the stakeholders. Those can be combined. Within reason, several courses of action are worth pursuing at the same time.

Step five -- Implementing the solution(s). Not much needs to be said here except that *people who solve problems together implement solutions together.* That is an axiom of any group process. It simply reflects the truism that students will do what *they* decide to do, not so much what others decide for them.

Teacher Art Sabiston found problems when his shop class regularly failed to clean up properly. After his collaboration ended, he wrote to me saying,

"The boys are cleaning without problems since they claimed ownership of the collaboration and accepted responsibility for cleaning relevant areas of the shop" (Sabiston, 2013, personal communication).

Step #6 – Course corrections/Following up. A good idea from the start is to monitor progress as the stakeholders move forward with their solution. This can be on a daily or weekly basis, or it can mean simply reconvening at a later date. At that time, the team can modify its solution, pick another solution, or set a time for further evaluating what's being done. More will be said about follow-up in chapter three.

HISTORIC ROOTS OF COLLABORATION:
THE CROW RITUAL

Native Americans lived in closer proximity than we do in modern America. Tribes can be presumed to have councils and other means of settling matters in dispute. Some even had elaborate rituals to celebrate peaceful methods, the following example coming from the Crow Nation. It lends a kinetic element to my workshops and can be acted out at home or in the classroom. When enacted in the classroom, the ritual seems to find a comfortable spot in children's memories.

The Crow rite-of-passage was to initiate young people into tribal membership. With the pre-teens waiting outside the tent or building, an elder would call one child into the tribe. There the juvenile would be told to face a second elder and join hands with his elder. Once they had joined hands at shoulder height, the two would be asked to push and shove without result. The presiding elder would ask the child, "Is that the way you want to solve problems with your brother?" Dutifully, the youngster would reply, "No."

The two would repeat the effort, but this time the elder would tumble backwards. "Is that the way you want to solve problems?" "No."

Finally, when the youngster shoved a third time, the elder would loop one hand over so that their hands, still clenched, were side by side. "Now where is your problem," the youngster was asked? Out in front. "Where is your vision?" Focused on the problem. "How are you standing?" Side by side. "Where are your shoulders?" They are touching, joined. Now the elder and the boy are shoulder-to-shoulder facing the symbol of their problem. Unfortunately, it is necessary to go back thousands of years to find a metaphor for collaborating, but there it is. Teachers can take this custom back to their classrooms both as a look at Native American folklore and as a beginning for understanding collaboration.

FACILITATING A SIX-STEP PROCESS

To repeat, the Gordon method is best learned as a neutral facilitator. In this way beginners can become comfortable with the steps and not have to protect a need of their own. In fact, facilitating without a neutral third party is a difficult and often misunderstood process. A closer look at two-party collaboration will be found in chapter three. For now, three party facilitation is the rule – the facilitator and two others we will call stakeholders, or simply *parties* committed to solving a problem.

First, the facilitator introduces the process. This is the set-up mentioned above. State the purpose (so that both will win), confirm the time frame in two parts (It this a good time? Is it enough time?) and ask if the parties are willing to try something new.

Once the set-up is complete, go directly to needs. (Do not ask "What do *you* think is the problem?" Such will derail your collaboration at the start.) Begin with the person who brought up the issue. This is simply a good-will gesture allowing that person to feel their appeal is getting the attention it deserves.

When listing needs, pay attention to notions the other party is likely to respect. Remember, the crosscheck is to get the parties side-by-side. But for now, only list the needs. You will want firm control of your process, and that is gained by guiding each sequence without letting one party get ahead. The rule-of-thumb is this: It is okay to go backwards in the steps but *not okay to get ahead*. This allows participants to modify their needs as they witness the collaborative effort helping out. It also lets the parties add solutions when they come to mind after step two is complete.

If one party does get ahead of the process, it is best to gently deflect the comment. When one person, say, offers a solution while I am assessing needs, I say "I know you'd like to see this (or that) solution. Remind me when we get to the step two. I will begin with your idea." This gentle handling of the disruption allows the facilitator to maintain their role as an effective listener while bringing the Gordon sequence back on line.

When assessing needs, pay attention to what I call "umbrella" statements – summaries that seem to encompass several spoken needs. For example, in a bullying situation, your response, "You need to feel safe," will normally cover several needs – the need not to be hit, the need not to be teased, not to be threatened, etc. Umbrella phrases also fill in one side of the collaboration equation in a manner that is hard to rebut. The bully has to understand his victim's need to feel safe or he will oust himself from the process.

Mutual understanding is completed with the crosscheck, which is that important transition between steps one and two. Only when the crosscheck is complete, when there is full acceptance of one another's needs, does solution finding come into play. Here the guidelines of brainstorming apply. Experienced mediators resist giving solutions at all costs. At this stage, the worst mistake facilitators can make is to give *the best solution*. Solving stakeholder's problems for them undermines ownership. It deflates the process in one innocent move. Poof!

As third-party facilitator, it is crucial to record key pieces of information: individual needs, the summary word (or phrase), the collaboration equation, solutions, evaluations, the eventual solution and assignments. The process ends when stakeholders agree on their assignment (or agree to continue later).

Here is the completed process submitted by a master's level student.

CASE STUDY:

What follows is a written assignment as facilitated and reported by Debbi Wallace. Her report is quoted verbatim. (Where the need is for emphasis, the italics are mine.)

THE PROBLEM

"This collaboration takes place between Monica and David, ten-year-old's in my fourth-grade classroom. They had been matched as partners for a cooperative learning activity. They were to choose a topic from the information on insects we'd been studying and present it to the class. They had been at a stalemate all morning as to how to present information on their chosen topic, 'How Crickets Sing.' They had asked for my help. I gave encouragement and suggested that they listen to each other's wishes. By 10 am, they were not talking at all.

"I perceived what I thought was their problem. This time I decided it would be a great time to use my facilitator skills to help them discover each other's needs. The following is an overview of what took place.

THE SET-UP

"I set things up informally as both agreed to use their library time to try this new process. They were anxious, but willing. We began with Monica stating her needs.

TROLLING FOR NEEDS

"Monica needed to get the work done, to have it look good, not to have to do all the work and to have fun.

"David's needs were much slower in coming and difficult for him to state. David needed to get it done, not get in trouble, and not miss recess and to have help. At this point, I repeated David's last comment to him. He said, "Yes, it's too hard." Monica reminded David that he had agreed to the topic of crickets. "I know but I don't want to write it." I wrote that on his list: David doesn't want to write.

"David added, "I can't read that stuff." I asked if he needed help in reading and he said he did. I wrote 'help with reading.' By now, Monica's face was wide-eyed with surprise and David was shifting in his chair.

"I introduced the needs equation. I reminded them that they would both be winners when we were done. Monica's side was easy for her to see. I led David through a slow questioning process (which Monica listened to intently) and in the end he stated his own need. The equation looked like this – *How could we finish the project so that Monica doesn't have all the work and David gets help and feels smart?*

"I checked with them, so they understood and accepted each other's need. Monica, especially, was very enthusiastic and supportive. "I didn't know what you needed!" she stated with a smile.

POSSIBLE SOLUTIONS

"From here on things went quickly. They easily created a list of solutions, rejected a few and came up with a plan. I spoke only a word or two and they did the rest.

1. Get an adult to help
2. Use drawings/diagrams
3. Monica writes and David draws
4. Do a game show

5. Monica reads and David picks important stuff to do (act out)
6. Make a video
7. Write a story about a cricket
8. Read together

CHOOSING THE SOLUTION

Monica put their basic ideas into a (combined) plan involving solutions two, three, five and eight. They could draw pictures showing the information and write a sentence with each one, explaining what it means. David added that he could act it out. "It would be funny," he said with a grin.

I had them tell me what they thought they should do next. They decided to read the book at the same time and Monica would write down the needed sentences. David would draw diagrams to go with the sentences and they would color them together. David also agreed to act out the part of a 'singing' cricket, much to Monica's relief! They both agreed to this solution and said they felt much better.

IMPLEMENTING THE SOLUTION(S)

"That afternoon, they were talking and listening to each other. Monica was eager to help David. He even had to back her off a bit. She asked for his opinion and he offered to help in many ways. Smiles were plentiful.

A note from teacher Debbi Wallace: "David has a learning disability and reads at a low first grade level. David is learning to express his needs and to work through his difficulties, not ignore them. This was a giant step for him. Monica, obviously, had no idea about David's weakness in reading. She is bright and sometimes quiet in new situations. If I had told them what they should do, David wouldn't have communicated his needs and Monica would have missed the chance to truly understand."

ONE NOTE OF CAUTION:

Debbi's job was to do more than guide the steps. She must take care to keep any aggressive remarks out of the needs assessment. She must translate whenever a need states a change in the other stakeholder's behavior. So, for *Monica needs David to help more*, Debbi would have written *Monica not have to do all the work*. Remember, it is Monica whose needs are being assessed. Likewise, among David's needs, for *Monica to help with reading*, Debbi would note *for David to get help with reading*. Using the passive voice to remain neutral is key to success.

During the needs assessment, particularly in an adversarial or competitive situation, the person who feels aggrieved will often demand the other party do (or stop doing) a certain behavior. If this is not corrected, it can lead back to bickering and re-ignite the disagreement. It takes experience to catch these traps and disable them, but it is not hard to do. Simply keep names out of the picture. The facilitator simply changes to the passive voice. When a facilitator hears, *"To get Frankie to stop hitting me,"* he or she repeats, *"For you to not be hit."* This will almost certainly lead to the deeper need, "To feel safe at school," and presto – you have a need the bully can sign off on... or lose his best chance to escape harsher resolution. The idea is to get a *NEEDS EQUATION* that both parties can accept. The best way to do that is to gently remove names from the assessment.

SUMMARY

Any negotiation that seeks to balance underlying needs is a collaboration. Any discussion based on superficial desires is a partnership, not a collaboration. When learning to collaborate, look for an issue that can be resolved as a neutral third party and one where full disclosure is expected. This keeps beginners focused on the process and not on the behavior of the participants. Make sure to complete the critical junctures cleanly and clearly and try not to proceed without those. They are the Set-Up and the Cross-Check. In both cases, one's instincts will tell whether the stakeholders are invested and ready to move forward.

With that in mind, return to Gordon's six-step method. Go through the steps one at a time, allowing parties to go back to an earlier step, but not forward, getting ahead of the process. Control the collaboration; do not control the people. For example, say, "Thanks. We will evaluate solutions when we get more ideas on the board. Meantime hold that thought. We'll need it when we measure solutions."

Translate aggressive comments so that they become innocuous to the other party. Simply change to the passive voice. This is best done by keeping names out of the assessment. Get closure to each collaboration or be exact about when it will continue. Get commitment to the solution from all stakeholders along with roles to be played when implementing the new idea.

Teachers are changing the power balance in their classrooms. They are demonstrating the truth of *to surrender power is to gain power*. They are finding children eager for collaborating to work, excited about one another and thrilled with the results.

Chapter 3

ADVANCED COLLABORATION

"First Your Pants, Then Your Shoes"

Gary Larson, The Far Side

If you thought collaboration's six-step process appears like conflict resolution, you would be right. However, many who study conflict are humbled and dismayed to learn how hard it is to deal with it in real life, especially when they are part of the dispute. For the most part, conflict resolution workshops demonstrate that resolution is *possible*; however, the art and science of conflict resolution is something left to the experts. Unless, of course, con-res is taught as a special case of collaboration. In that case, it is simply an aftermarket bolt-on to the basic design.

Imagine a stream running along a map until it reaches a bridge. But the bridge, symbolizing conflict, is destroyed, and has fallen into the water to block traffic. Now imagine that upstream of the damage, there lies conflict resolution. Upstream of that lies conflict *prevention* and still farther upstream one finds problem solving. Further upstream of problem solving is problem prevention and further than that, routine decision-making. The purpose of chapter 2 has been to introduce problem solving along the collaborative model, but also to enable teachers and staff to adopt a vocabulary that keeps the focus on human needs. As such, the previous chapter provides a structure for ordinary deciding. Safety of individual

Teachers are changing the power balance in their classrooms. They are demonstrating the truth of *to surrender power is to gain power*. They are finding children eager for collaborating to work, excited about one another and thrilled with the results.

Chapter 3

ADVANCED COLLABORATION

"First Your Pants, Then Your Shoes"

Gary Larson, The Far Side

If you thought collaboration's six-step process appears like conflict resolution, you would be right. However, many who study conflict are humbled and dismayed to learn how hard it is to deal with it in real life, especially when they are part of the dispute. For the most part, conflict resolution workshops demonstrate that resolution is *possible*; however, the art and science of conflict resolution is something left to the experts. Unless, of course, con-res is taught as a special case of collaboration. In that case, it is simply an aftermarket bolt-on to the basic design.

Imagine a stream running along a map until it reaches a bridge. But the bridge, symbolizing conflict, is destroyed, and has fallen into the water to block traffic. Now imagine that upstream of the damage, there lies conflict resolution. Upstream of that lies conflict *prevention* and still farther upstream one finds problem solving. Further upstream of problem solving is problem prevention and further than that, routine decision-making. The purpose of chapter 2 has been to introduce problem solving along the collaborative model, but also to enable teachers and staff to adopt a vocabulary that keeps the focus on human needs. As such, the previous chapter provides a structure for ordinary deciding. Safety of individual staff members, particularly emotional safety, depends on this type of teaming in the school. Fundamental to the desired context is to bargain over the *shared problem* and never over entrenched positions (Fisher and Ury, 1981, p. 38).

First we will examine what happens to the collaborative moment when parties will not reveal their needs. Other advanced scenarios occur when the collaborating parties are hostile, when there is both anger and hidden agenda, when there are multiple parties to the negotiations, and those difficult moments when there is no neutral person to mediate. In that case, the skilled party must protect his needs while also facilitating the event. The schematic shown below illustrates how incremental training proceeds.

Collaborating with Hidden Needs

Throughout chapter 2, we have assumed full disclosure on the part of A and B. More than that, we have assumed novice facilitators will first attempt the Gordon process as a neutral facilitator. This allows them to be uninterested in outcomes, and able to focus on the problem-solving sequence. The next development would be facilitating when the parties do not reveal their needs. This is represented by the dashed line connecting parties A and B (below).

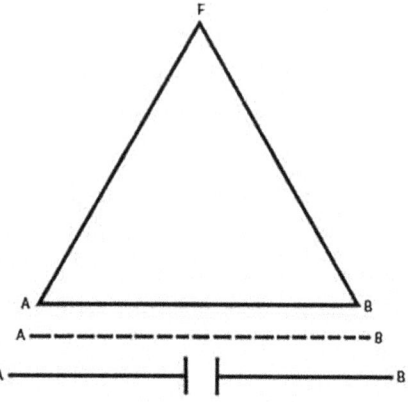

SIDEBAR

The diagram above shows the teaching model used in my classroom as well as in this book. Training in collaboration is designated to be incremental, developmental so that information builds on that which is already known

Here, A and B are parties to the collaboration represented by the straight line at the bottom of triangle. The (neutral) facilitator is designed F. The dashed line represent parties holding a hidden agenda and the 'blocked' and final line indicates conflict.

When collaborating amid hidden needs, the facilitator must dredge up those needs so that they can be winnowed down to the collaborative equation. Recall from the previous chapter that needs start out as basic to human existence, then become more sublime as one progresses through life. Unmet needs, then, dictate where parties A and B are entering the process. The way to bring them into play is to listen. Active listening means hearing what is said and communicating to participants that they are being attended to, in other words, heard. School teachers, thanks to decades of emphasis, are perfectly adept (in cross section) at active listening. They practice it every day. They teach children how to listen, perhaps not as directly as in the Gordon method. Their teaching is by example. Listening engenders trust in the process --

Collaborative Leadership for the Classroom

equally important to helping uncover hidden needs. Listen effectively and you will get the required buy-in from participants.

I am indebted to consultant David Landsburg of Tucson, Arizona for his *NON-DIRECTIVE LISTENING FOR MANAGERS*, the most succinct short-form of instruction I am aware of. Below is the Landsburg handout, inserted here with permission.

O-COMM CONCEPTS

Non-Directive Listening for Managers

Research studies suggest that the number one subordinate complaint about managers is that they do not listen. Part of the reason for those findings is that, indeed, managers may not listen enough. Another part of the reason is that managers may not give enough feedback to their employees indicating that they are trying to listen.

Carl Rogers developed a counseling technique which is called either "Active Listening" or "Non-directive listening." It is based on the concept that a counselor or psychologist can help a client solve his problem by listening to him in a non-directive manner. This same approach can be used by managers to help employees solve their own problems. Such a practice encourages personal growth on the part of employees. It also means that employees are more apt to buy into the solution, since they developed it themselves.

Rules

The following list of six rules gives a basic overview of the non-directive listening process.

1. **Take time** to listen carefully. Non-directive listening cannot be hurried. If you have an important appointment in a few minutes, do not start non-directive listening. Instead, set an appointment to deal with the problem at a later time.

2. **Be attentive** to the employee. Concentrate your total attention on what the employee is saying.

3. **Give three verbal reactions.** Those reactions are all designed to show the employee that you are trying to understand what is being said. Yet, you do not want to direct the conversation. The reactions are silence (the employee will usually fill the silence by telling you more), intelligent grunts (such as "uh huh") which say I understand, but still do not direct the conversation, and paraphrasing, which involves repeating what you heard in terms of both content and feelings.

4. **Use no aggressive probes.** Your natural curiosity will often cause you to want to ask specific questions to get more information. However, that makes you the director and reduces the probability that the employee will solve the problem himself.

5. **Never evaluate** what the employee is telling you. You do not disagree with him. Nor, do you say you support his opinion. Employees will often want your opinion. However, if you give

> them an opinion, you begin to direct them in the problem solving process. This may not be in their best interest.
>
> 6. **Never lose faith** in the ability of the employee to solve the problem. The principle on which this system works is that people can solve their own problems. By solving the problem herself, the employee becomes more committed to making the solution work, and at the same time develops problem solving skills.
>
> The underlying principle is that the manager should give lots of feedback which says to the employee that "I really want to understand what you are saying."
>
> When to Use
>
> Using this technique will get you high marks from employees who want their managers to listen to them more. It might also improve employee commitment to the task. However, the total technique cannot be used in all situations. Consider the following four factors when deciding whether or not to use non-directive listening in any specific situation.
>
> 1. Confirm that you are discussing a **complex problem**. It is probably not worth getting into the process if the employee just wants to know whether to use form A or form B.
>
> 2. Make certain you have the **necessary time and commitment** to go through the process. It is not wise to start the non-directive listening process, only to cut the conversation short to move on to a more important matter.
>
> 3. Be sure that you can **withhold judgement** on the issue. It is admirable to help employees in solving problems. However, you must be able to live with whatever solution is selected. If the employee is trying to decide whether or not it is appropriate to drink alcohol at lunch time, there may be company policy which already makes the decision.
>
> 4. Only use the process **in proportion**. Employees will grow very tired of intelligent grunts and nodding silence if you use the technique all the time.
>
> Americans are feeling increasingly alienated -- from neighbors, from families, from companies. People are looking for someone who will listen to them -- someone to whom they can be committed. By using some portion or all of the process of non-directive listening, you can help employees solve their own problems, increase their commitment to the company and increase their commitment to you as a manager.
>
> Incidentally, the same principles work for salespeople, especially during the interview phase when you are trying to discover the customer's felt needs.

DAVID L. LANDSBURG

9160 E. Holmes • Tucson, Arizona 85710

(602) 885-1602

One technique missing from Landsburg's approach is a device for encouraging participants to open up – it is the upward inflection of a spoken word, indicating that one is asking a question. Effective facilitators will choose a key word (or phrase) and simply repeat it using an upward tilt. For example, one party to the collaborative might say, "I didn't know it was that far away." Try saying, "That far away?" "Yes, because it will take me longer to get there." "Take longer?" "I can't get away early. I'm afraid I'll walk in late."

People enjoy being attended to. This simple maneuver helps them get in touch with hidden needs and articulate them to the facilitator. It also builds trust, both in the facilitator and the process. Of course, one might say, "Tell me more about that . . . ", or "Say more on that. . . " Nevertheless, as indicated by Landsburg's title, active listening tends to be more non-directive. On the other hand, a steady diet of listening can irritate. So be ready to alternate with a direct approach. Just know that you are there to build trust. And remember, your purpose from the beginning is to see that both sides (of the collaboration) win.

AN EXAMPLE OF FACILITATING
WITH UNSPOKEN NEEDS

A local Kiwanis club was weeks away from installing new officers when the outgoing and incoming presidents, together with myself, were caucusing to develop fresh ideas. The new president -- I'll call him Allan -- suggested changing the first meeting of the month to a general meeting rather than a director's meeting, as had been the long-standing tradition. This meant coming up with a schedule for board meetings outside the accepted monthly practice. The old president we'll call Jim.

Jim: "I can tell you, I'd be against a change like that."
Allan: "Why? I want to give that 1st morning back to the general membership."

Jim: "I'm just against it. I see no reason for the change."
Me: (after a few minutes of the same) "Would you guys mind if I facilitated here?" I went through the checklist for opening a collaboration, ending with my purpose to see that both men would be taken care of. They agreed.
Me: "Allan, what are your needs around shifting that first meeting over to the members?"
Allan: "Meetings are fun. I want to share them with the rest, like every week."
Me: "What does it do for you to extend that initial meeting to everybody?"
Allan: "I don't know."
Me: "What would it be if you did know?" (Another gambit on my part)
Allan: "I'm not sure." (Gambit failed)
Me: "Jim, what do you need around these meetings?"
Jim: "I need things to stay the way they are."
Me: "You're content with the status quo."
Jim: "Well, sure. I can't come to a separate board meeting no matter when."
Me: "Can't come?"
Jim: "I travel farthest anyway. I just can't add one more meeting."
Me: "So it's economical – just travel to three meeting a month plus one board meeting."
Jim: "Yes."
Me: "Let's enter that in the collaboration equation – Jim needs to economize his travels.
Allan, have you identified your need around changing it up?"

Allan: "I think I would like to identify myself as caring about the membership, about making a decision that favors their interests."

Me: "We can enter that. But it seems as if we have a third party to these negotiations. How do we know what members want?"

Jim: "I don't know of any dissatisfaction with the way things are. Why not see what the members want?"

At this point, we agreed to the collaboration equation – HOW CAN WE meet Jim's need for economizing his travel SO THAT we meet Allan's need for acting in favor of the group? Next on our agenda would be to raise the question in front of the membership. [In fact, private conversations showed no one actually wanted four open meetings. The issue was dropped, saving Allan from raising a question he could not pursue.]

COLLABORATING WITH ANGRY PEOPLE

With the way Allan and Jim started out, I am sure things would have disintegrated to where they became heated. Jim already had dug in his heels with "If you change the board meeting, I won't come to it." and Allan had frustrated both Jim and I for not being able to identify his need. But what do facilitators do when issues begin to go up in flames?

COLLABORATING WHEN ANGER IS PRESENT

Let's go back to the beginning for a moment. In your set-up, you will need to add a key ingredient if anger is present or even anticipated. This is the one rule that governs collaboration; there are no others. *Only one person can talk at a time.* I call this The Angry Rule. My suggestion is not to invoke it if aggressive feelings are not on the horizon. My reasoning is people are hounded by enough rules, and they can only open up if they are free of them, even if just for the moment. Once again, the Angry Rule is part of the set-up, and only needs to be mentioned if anger is present. [Facilitating amid anger is symbolized by the communication blockage between A and B in the diagram (page 54). F continues as the neutral facilitator.]

By this time in the incremental sequence, we are at conflict resolution, but we have arrived by a very different route. By treating con-res as a special case of collaboration, we can assume there is an overlay of skilled communication in place in your classroom or school building. This makes resolving conflict one of the easiest of problems to confront. Three reasons for this are; 1) followers are comfortable with the collaborative overlay, and are eager to get back to it, 2) despite the urban myth that people love to fight, they actually like resolution, and 3) angry people will tell you what they need. You will simply need a recipe for turning the anger around to where it works in your favor. Before you do that, you can profit from what every professional counselor has carved in stone on her desk – *Hear the feelings first!* Let's go to another example.

Teacher and coach Steven Johnson describes what happens when conflict erupts between two girls, affecting the performance of his volleyball team. "Nikki and Tonya are normally friends. They played together for the previous three years. When catty remarks occurred in the past, I would attempt to solve the problem using an authoritarian approach, 'All right ladies, what's the problem? Here is the solution, now get back to practice.'"

Thirty minutes into practice, Nikki said, "You could have gotten that ball if you would just more your feet."

INTRODUCTION: I called Tonya and Nikki over and expressed my concern about the friction that was developing between them, and that I wanted to help them both get their needs met. When I asked if it was a good time, both girls said no; they wanted to keep on with practice but could stay afterward to work on the issue.

After practice I repeated my concern and asked if they were willing to try a new process that will allow them both to get their needs met. Both agreed. I then told them that in order for the process to work, only one person can talk at a time. Again, they both agreed.

Steven: "Tonya, let's begin with you. What are your needs?"
Tonya: (Animated) "I need the coach to provide feedback, not Nikki"
Steven: "You feel strongly that I'm the one to give criticism."
Tonya: "Yes. And I need Nikki to treat me with respect."
Nikki: (Talking over) "But how can I respect you if you don't support me in the games?"
Steven: (With hand up to Nikki) "Nikki, remember. We'll get to your needs in a moment."

Nikki:	(Nods)
Steven:	(To Tonya) "It's respect then, isn't it? You need to be respected on the floor."
Tonya:	"Not just in volleyball, all the time."
Steven:	"I understand."

I then asked Nikki to assess her needs.

Nikki:	"I need Tonya to support me in games and in practice."
Steven:	'You need to be supported."
Nikki:	"Yes, and I need Tonya to give me a chance to give input when the team is in a huddle."
Steven:	"Input in the huddle?"
Nikki:	"Yes. You know, when we huddle up. That's when Tonya cuts me off. She has a bad habit."
Steven:	"So it happens regularly. And that makes you mad."
Nikki:	"Well, sure."
Steven:	"Do I understand, Nikki, that you need support from the team and to give input in the huddle?"

Nikki concurred. I then asked Tonya if she understood what Nikki was saying and if it was okay for her to take that stance?

Tonya:	"I understand, and it is okay."
Steven:	(Turning to Tonya) "And do I understand that I am the only one to give coaching feedback?"

I turned to Nikki and asked if she understood what Tonya was saying and was it okay. Nikki understood and said it was okay.

Steven:	"So how can Nikki feel free to give input to the team and receive verbal support for her efforts so that Tonya can feel free of peer

criticism and be respected?" Once both girls acknowledged their needs were valid, the brainstorming process began. Alternating, Nikki and Tonya offered solutions.

Nikki's solutions: Not to coach Tonya
    To support Tonya's efforts and suggestions
    To have she and Tonya pair up during partner drills

Tonya's solutions: Not to speak in team huddles until everyone has a chance to talk
    To verbally encourage the team during practice and games

    The girls agreed that they wanted to implement all of the solutions. They understood my wanting to pair them up only sometimes out of concern for the interaction that occurs among the team. The girls agreed to meet one week later to assess how their solutions were working and if any adjustments need to be made.

CONCLUSION:

Since taking this class and implementing the principles with Nikki and Tonya I can now see that the authoritarian approach is counterproductive and negatively impacts team chemistry. By facilitating the process, the girls were able to communicate their needs with a neutral party and have them validated by the other person. I was initially surprised that they didn't come up with solutions that the other would find disagreeable. However, after giving the process some thought, I concluded that the solutions suggested were reasonable and accepted because the girls first acknowledged the other's needs. Finally, my stress level remains low as the participants become the problem solvers.

What makes a person angry? He or she has suffered a loss. Here is where you make anger work in your favor. Angry people will tell you their loss; what's missing is their gain. Presto – Now you have the need for one side of the collaboration equation. By ameliorating feelings, you will have brought the parties to where they can be assertive with each other.

Aggressive postures do hinder effective communication, at least until a facilitator or moderator steps in to hear the anger, settle it, and uncover the underlying need. Aggressive behavior says, "You're stupid." Passive behavior suggests, "I'm stupid." Think of assertive behavior as neither passive nor aggressive. Forget the rulebook on how to become assertive. Simply 'translate' B's aggression into words which A can accommodate. One way to do this is to change from the active to the passive voice. For example, when Johnny says, "Sandra keeps teasing me," your response can be, "You don't like being teased." Shifting to the passive voice keeps Sandra's name out of the picture temporarily, long enough for her to sit still with your statement. Remember, if Sandra erupts here, remind her that only one can speak at a time.

Enforcing the Angry Rule can be as light as a hand held up to the offending party, reminding him about the Angry Rule, saying "I can't help you if both are taking at the same time," threatening to abort the process if they continue talking over one another, and finally, asking, "What would you like to happen now?" Facilitators occupy a powerful position in the collaboration. Parties A and B *do not want that power;* it means the end of problem solving. I have seen situations where the disputants willingly give power back to their facilitator, and I have even experienced it in a life-threatening moment of my own.

Ten years ago, I was jogging on Seattle's Queen Anne Hill when a youngster lying flat on his skateboard went flashing down through traffic, narrowly missing a car turning into his path. I instinctively grasped the arm of one of his less foolish friends as he tramped past, with, "Hey! Your friend could have been killed. Tell him not to skateboard on this hill." The young man jerked his arm away and when I reached the bottom of the hill, three of them blocked me into a dead-end corner of a park. No one was there to witness as they jabbed their boards within inches of my face, threatening to kill me if I touched one of them again.

Foolishly, I tried to tough the moment out. I remembered a movie line Gene Hackman used to get out of a tight spot. I confronted the talker, "You got a pretty good attorney?" "Yeah," he barked, "I got three of them and they just got me out. Same as they'll do next time."

I couldn't dig myself in any deeper, so I went belly up. I sat on a rock abutment. They mustn't see my knees shaking. *"What do you want to happen now?"* The situation immediately evaporated! Their leader backed off, lowering his board. The others did the same, while chiming in absent mindedly, "We'll get you old man," and "Don't you worry." They strode away, leaving me a confused bundle of nerves.

The truth of the matter is this: your conflict resolution will never get as far as my misadventure so long as you introduce a collaborative overlay in your classroom, school, or even workplace. In chapter 4, we will look at any number of interventions that can (situationally) take the place of collaboration. In the meantime, know that collaborating using a neutral third-party facilitator is the last, best place for those involved in a dispute. This is even truer when staff members are known to collaborate and do so in smaller ways every day. By this time in your journey, everyone is watching, certainly the children in your school.

COLLABORATING WITHOUT A THIRD-PARTY FACILITATOR

Guiding a collaboration while 'owning' part of the problem is hard. Nevertheless, experienced facilitators – those who can profit from experience as a neutral mediator – will find they can conquer the challenge without much difficulty. The diagram below shows a schematic of what this facilitation looks like, moving from full disclosure through hidden agenda and ending with conflict. Party A (or B) plays the facilitator. The absence of a third party is obvious.

COLLABORATIVE LEADERSHIP FOR THE CLASSROOM

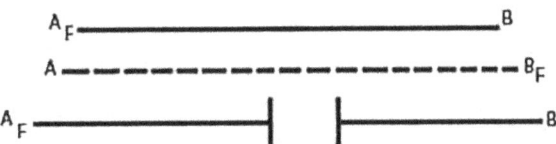

SIDEBAR

This diagram shows the more advanced training model where an neutral facilitator is not present. The role of 'F' must be played by the party with skill in that area, either A or B. Once again, training in collaboration is designed to be incremental, developmental.

THis normally requires practice as a third party facilitator. It is a difficult way to learn because one's counterpart to the collaboration might view neutral behavior as a weakness. 'Changing hats' as Gordon called it is neither for the timid nor for the beginner

In the following case study, teacher Charlene Ponsford describes a conflict collaboration between herself and a 5th grade student.

Situation: Brian would often from recess and yell put-downs at other students or call them cheaters. This occurred in the first few days of school. At first, I just reminded Brian that put-downs are not allowed, and that people do not like being called a cheater. However, this just didn't work. I asked Brian if he would see me after lunch to work out a solution to the problem.

Setting the Stage: I explained to Brian that we have a problem and that I would like to solve it in a way we would both feel good. Brian seemed to be relaxed with the suggestion. Both of us sat in a student desk facing each other. I leaned forward with paper and pen in hand. I then explained I had taken a class for teachers designed to help solve situations where both people are happy with the outcome. I asked his permission to use the strategy. He replied, "Sure," gesturing with both hands, turning them over and open. (This signaled to me his trust, so I felt good about proceeding).

OOPS: I forgot to ask if this is a good time and if he felt we had enough time.

Defining the Problem: I told Brian I wanted to write down our conversation because it was important and because we may need to look back on it later. I then told him that each of us will express our concerns around the situation, and then we would think about solutions. At the end we would pick solutions we are both happy with. Brian responded with a confident "OK."

Charlene: "Brian, I'll start first telling you what I need, and then I'll listen to what you need. Is that OK?"
Brian: "Sure."
Charlene: "What I need is for the class to feel safe from put-downs. They hurt peoples' feelings. You can understand that."
Brian: "I know."

Charlene: "So, Brian, what is your need? What do you want?"
Brian: "Well, Jesse, Bubba, David, and Charles are cheating at recess playing football."
Charlene: "Ah, so I see now why you are so frustrated when you come in from recess. It's important to you that people are playing the game fairly or it's no fun."
Brian: "Yeah, that's why I called Charles a cheater."
Charlene: "So Charles is the problem?"
Brian: "Not so much as the other three. He only does it because other kids cheat. If they didn't cheat Charles wouldn't."
Charlene: "How are those other kids Bubba, Jesse, and David failing to play fairly?"
Brian: "When they have the ball and get touched, they keep on running."
Charlene: "You mean they don't go down once they're tagged? They just keep on running even though the play is over? It bothers you that that's unfair."
Brian: "Yup."
Charlene: "OK Brian, your need is for fair play. When the boys get touched, they should go down and end the play."
Brian: "Yes."

Needs Equation and Cross Check?

Charlene: "Is there anything you want to add?"
Brian: "No."
Charlene: "Great! I think we have all the information. Before we begin to think of ways we can both get what we need, I want to be sure

	we understand each other's needs. Brian, do you understand and see why I have the need for no hurt feelings in our classroom?"
Brian:	"Yeah, sure."
Charlene:	"Great! Your need is to have the others play fair football, going down when they are touched. I can understand your need."
Brian:	"Well, it's not all the time. Most of the time they play fair. It's just on some plays they cheat."
Charlene:	"Oh, OK it's just sometimes."
Brian:	"Yeah."

Creative Solution: After brainstorming with Brian, we decided he would no longer use put-downs to solve his problem with recess. I would talk with the other boys' 6th grade teacher suggesting he say something like, "You boys are doing a pretty good job of playing football, but occasionally you are not ending the play when you are tagged. It would be better if you always went down when tagged." We agreed that Brian's name would be kept confidential because the older boys might turn on him. If unfair play continued, we could ask the principal to speak with the boys. If the problem still existed, we could expand the collaboration to include the other three boys.

Conclusion: It has only been two days, but there were no incidents. Brian is a troubled child with a difficult background. I'm not confident his outbursts will end because Brian uses this behavior to cope. What did happen is Brian and I are building a trusting relationship where we can work to improve his coping skills. Brian felt important in our conversation. For me, I believe in this process. It allowed me to understand Brian's name calling was not an attack on my authority, but a cry for help by a child with a need who doesn't know how to express it nor fulfill it. We are all better off thanks to this process.

Chapter 4

SITUATIONAL LEADERSHIP REVISITED

Collaborative Leadership and the Industrial Hierarchy "I was an oak. Now I'm a willow. I can bend."

Sung by Elvis Presley

Lao Tzu was no clairvoyant. When he wrote, "A leader is best when people barely know he exists," the ancient sage could not have seen the appearance of education in 2019 (Heider, 1986). High Stakes testing challenges students while exhausting them at the same time. On the one hand, charter schools are undermining the roots of public education. On the other, taxpayers demand accountability. Worse, Margaret Thatcher's enigmatic *Consensus is the negation of leadership* has enough devotees to steer collaboration straight into the jaws of conflict (Thatcher, 2004). Today, teachers find themselves with bulls-eyes on their backs and leadership as dizzying a task as they have faced. Hubris notwithstanding, the dean at a prominent northwest teaching university solves his dilemma this way: "There is one way to lead around here. Mine!" (Personal communication of January 2012)

Leadership! Socrates had trouble with it. So did Obama. So too, does Trump. Now, with charter schools, voucher programs, and right-wing interests such as Eli Broad and the Koch brothers wanting a piece of the action, today's teacher faces tasks more capricious than most can imagine. Dredging up solutions is taxing. Implementing them is exhausting. Satisfying constituencies is improbable. Obtaining loyalty is hair-raising. Education is under siege.

Here are examples from our nation's schools: For appointing a committee, one principal ignites defiance. No! he is told, *You decide and tell us.* To settle a difference among staff, a fellow teacher gets 'dissed'; *You're not telling us who is right.* In a school where some thirty issues are unresolved, an entire staff grumbles about leadership-by-default. They complain, we would never be in charge here. *Never! You couldn't pay us enough.*

What happens when a leader confronts her uncertain footing head-on? Principal Gerri Harmon was prudent about her new assignment. *Be decisive right from the start.* She paced her campus, and then cut fifteen minutes off the working day. Were her teachers impressed? They filed a grievance overnight. *"What's the difference*, she grimaces, *I'm doing what I did at my last school. These teachers will not let me take charge"* (Personal communication, 2014).

Today there are many reasons why leading is different. Some-- self-esteem training, assertiveness and empowerment -- were put in place by educators. As ironic as it is fitting, teachers must oversee the boisterous free-for-all which results.

A single reason, however, stands above the rest. In the years since Harmon passed a similar initiation in a nearby district, the hierarchy has flattened. Corporate America manipulated the flattening by slashing middle managers and plowing savings into The Bottom Line (Daft, R. L., 2013). For teachers, this progression does not exist. For them, a flattened hierarchy means more than truncated chains of command. It means, suitably enough, that authority-for-authority's sake is dead. With independent expression encouraged, educators must listen, harmonize and synthesize, all without resorting to power. Until we learn to do this, followers will continue to thrust ideas, but with little respect for the other guy's ideas. So, while nobody wants to be the leader, everyone wants to lead.

Face-to-face with Harmon, and with no glib fix in mind, I stalled. "You're hurt by this lack of support," I stumbled. "Well, of course!" An anguished look spread over Harmon's cautious decorum. "I don't want control all the time," she pleaded, "I just want some control some of the time" (Personal communication, 2016).

With hierarchical models breaking down, many classroom teachers feel the same as Harmon. When do they need control and how much control do they need? Bart Simpson comes alive in every classroom and teachers must dance to his tune, balancing command-and-control with respect for the verboseness of every child.

Hersey/Blanchard: The Reigning Standard

For thirty years, the melding of authority with participative decision-making has been the domain of Paul Hersey and Ken Blanchard, originators of a bell curve they named Situational Leadership. Hersey/Blanchard argued that traditional leading, based on codes of accountability and the power to punish and reward, can be adjusted according to stages of group cohesion. As shown in Figure #1 (counterclockwise from bottom right), the situational leader decides less as the subordinate group matures (Hersey, 1984).

THE FOUR LEADERSHIP STYLES

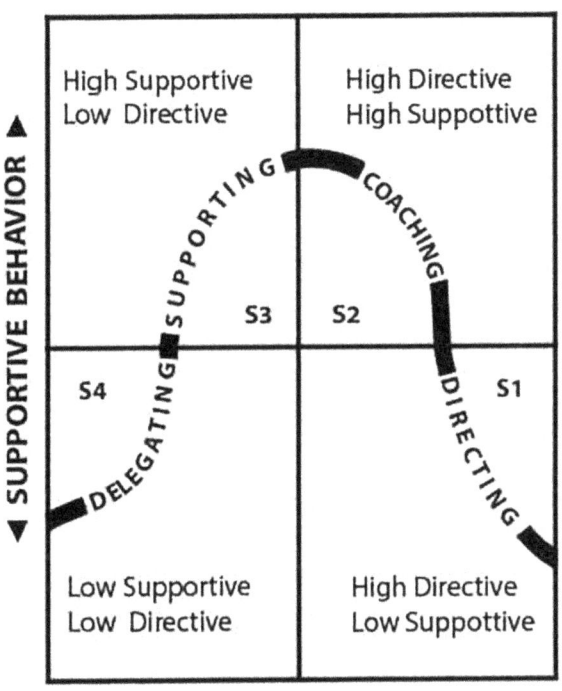

Figure 1 Source: Hersey, P.

Situational Leadership can be readily applied in schools. At many universities, Hersey/ Blanchard permeates graduate training for teachers. Small wonder! Group membership, finite work periods, the incremental nature of learning, independent tasks, the autonomy of teachers and the learning needs of students – all are elements more patterned and more predictable than in the modern workplace. Schools would seem an ideal incubator for Hersey/Blanchard leading. In many cases they are.

Yet, like the leading it promotes, Situational Leadership can itself be modified, adjusted to meet classroom realities. Hersey/Blanchard rests on internal measures – trust, bonding, knowledge, industry, and heart. Today, we can amplify Hersey/Blanchard so that it recognizes forces acting upon the group as well as those within. In today's schools, where prerogatives reflect the insistence of corporations, parents, ethnic groups, politicians, and even self-assured moral voices, internal measures are not enough. Neither is it acceptable for leaders to subjectively assess their group's maturity. This *definitive* quality of leadership is what grates.

Needed is a way to balance authority with participation, to meld collaborative leading with command-and-control. Yet as Jurist Michael Josephson years ago lamented, "We stubbornly try to force authority to make some compromise with participation, and without success" (Josephson with Bill Moyers, 1988).

Situational Leadership Revisited

What happens when we chart leadership methods not according to group development, rather by the number of people who decide? If we accept Thomas Gordon's thesis that the terms leadership and problem-solving are interchangeable, we pop through Alice's rabbit lair into uncharted landscapes indeed (Gordon, 1977: p 27). Just as there are many ways to solve problems, there are many ways to lead.

To match leader methods to events in the classroom, first create a spectrum, or 'menu' of styles (Figure 2). Compromising, voting, commanding, collaborating, and consulting are all methods for deciding. Authority serves as the pole on the left. One hundred percent participation (for example, jury deliberations) becomes the pole on the right.

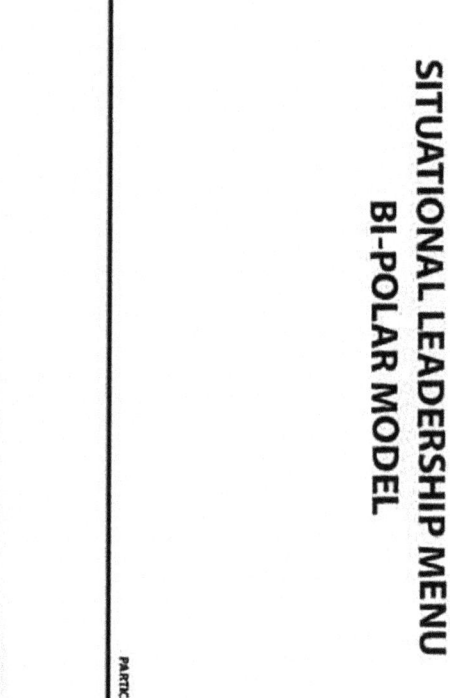

Figure 2 Source: The Author

By arranging leader interventions along the resulting chart, teachers can adjust their style to match events. Their behavior then flexes with circumstances, perhaps shifting so rapidly that methods appear to overlap. Teacher Mary Shaw, for example, returned from recess to shouts from every fourth grader in her class (personal communication, 2013). The use of the school basketball had triggered a dispute with another class. Mary opened the divider between classes (decided) supervised the choice of speakers (voted), and then facilitated (mediated) between factions. The two classes not only spoke through their delegates (democracy), they caucused (consulted) at times among themselves. Practiced Flex Leaders not only recognize these shifts, they foster them – and begin the delicate balance of participation with command-and-control.

The Role of Personal Values

Before teachers can adopt such a variable model, a refresher in facilitation skills will help. However, they face a more daunting task – defining their essence as leaders. Faced with a multifaceted approach, teachers can profit by determining which styles are compatible with their individual mindsets and goals. As never before, they need to be clear about personal values.

Since teachers have different values, their individual menus will differ, becoming unique to the character and goals of each. While this precludes a universal leader template, it also requires teachers to develop their own templates. Unlike bosses who stand on authority, today's educators must do nothing less than discover, then honor their own uniqueness.

To be proactive when choosing styles, teachers must have a grip on their values. For teachers to be recognized according to their dynamic along the chart (as opposed to how they wield authority), they need to put aside appearances and allow themselves to be known. Most teachers will be content with five or six favorite interventions. Once the menu pattern of the teacher becomes recognizable, energy and enthusiasm infuse the classroom and even school.

Key Indicators: Impact and Concern

To guide Flex Leading among in-touch and vocal students, teachers will serve their interests by including one set of measures not found in Hersey/Blanchard – impact and concern. After decades of uneven reform, impact and concern remain the hottest buttons in education today. When pushed, they inflame entire communities, especially when decisions roll down from the top. They are the *hit* and *hurt* of modern leading.

Impact and concern will continue to transform teacher leadership. These two factors clamor for attention when decisions are made across the land. For example, to the question of who shall decide, we might ask: Who is affected? Who cares? Who has information we need? What degree of trust exists among the group? What priorities need attention? How much time do we have? School reformers agree: To accomplish such alchemy, effective leadership begs to consider the concerns of those who put decisions to work.

When teachers consciously address these measures, the scope of their leading changes. The question is no longer how much authority to use. Rather, should authority be used at all? With which of many methods shall I intervene? These questions divide leadership into a two-step sequence, requiring teachers to first determine how a decision is to be reached. Because flexible leading affects buy-in, matching leadership style with circumstance is more important than the wisdom of the actual decision. This example is another way of saying that what is decided is not as important as all students accepting the solution and putting their shoulders to the wheel.

The Bi-Polar Option

In Figure 2, teachers can select not from one style (authority), but from seven styles. Some are based in authority and some in participation. Since authority-based leading involves one decision maker, the diagram shows authority on the left. Increasing the number of deciders moves the reader's imagination to the right. Of the disciplines shown, five are traditional. Pure participation is vague and as such, problematic. Collaborative leading, despite much rhetoric, remains innovative. Because it has the structure lacking in random participation, collaborating becomes the *operative* pole on the right.

Adding styles now completes the framework, a menu ordered by the number of people who decide. Some styles are harder to place than others. Collaboration, for example, might be placed anywhere except at the pole on the left. In general, collaboration is a peer model of deciding, shunning authority, and rank. Sometimes confused with collegiality or consensus, it is a process for *reaching* consensus. In general, two people can collaborate. So can an entire class. Since so many individuals might be involved, collaboration is shown nearer the pole on the right. Once collaboration is decided upon, each teacher will begin to involve students based on his or her values. Are the students affected? Are they concerned? Do students have information the teacher needs? Do students want a voice? Can students trust the others? Do they trust their teacher? Or, does the teacher already have a solution in mind? Predetermined solutions spell trouble for would-be collaborators. Leaders who obscure their decision-making power while mouthing the jargon of collaboration have difficulty without equal, even among raw authoritarians. They place themselves at a high-risk position – top left along the chart. (Figure 3)

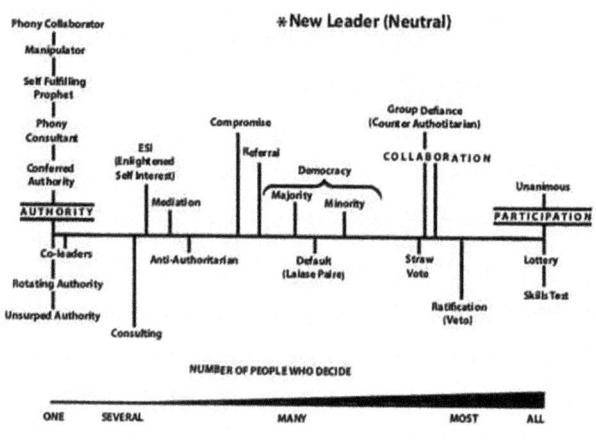

NON-NEGOTIABLE STYLES of LEADERSHIP -Collusion & Alliance, Criminal Indictment, Civil Litigation, Binding Arbitration, Force (including war), Deception/Stealt, Injunction, Restraining Order, Intimidation, Threat of any above

© 12/89 (Revised January 1993)

Figure 3 Source: The Author

Trust for the Process

Trust for the process might come slowly. Where trust is present, children eagerly share solutions and ideas. Children are naturals here. They sense when to speak up, how to stay within the boundaries of each style, and when they are legitimately excluded from debate. Wonderfully prepared by decades of classroom innovation -- assertiveness training, active listening, and self-esteem -- children are ideally suited for the features of the Bi-Polar chart.

When teachers use the flexible model, the model itself generates trust. Trust increases regard for the model, resulting in reciprocity, just as with any mutual connection. Two years into flexible leading, Principal Lynn Roberts was astonished when two teachers asked to combine their curricula. "These two weren't even speaking with one another before we adopted the Bi-Polar model" (Roberts, personal communication, 2013).

"It's Under My Control"

Different teachers find different rewards. Flexible leading gives vice principal and school counselor Katherine Palmer a different reward – confidence. "I found a way to blend my two roles. It's okay to move from one end of the chart to the other. It's under my control." (Palmer, personal communication, 2011).

Beyond flexing among styles, it is when implementing where miracles seem commonplace. In the classroom, teacher Raymond Salinas' collaboration resulted in students generating their own criteria for grading group presentations. Salinas reports:

It's been a couple of days since my students devised their plan and implemented it. Watching my students has been refreshing. I see them working harder than normal, being more responsible for their learning and having a better attitude for their work. Also that work is much better than what it had been before. I notice a sense of pride. (Salinas, personal communication, 2015).

Teachers like Salinas do more than guide effective solutions. They transform the construct of power in the classroom and provide a framework to resolve similar problems in the future.

Authority Here to Stay

For children to become effective leaders themselves, they need exposure to many leadership styles. By demonstrating from among some two dozen interventions (Fig 3), teachers can show a reasonable complement of participatory methods without surrendering their authority. Indexing to one allows that authority-based leading has its place. Teachers reluctant to share power have their own integrity; they simply have different values. With Flex Leading, no teacher needs to change. However, for men and women comfortable with authority, that fact may be best acknowledged. In today's world, acknowledging the tendency toward command-and-control may take more courage than learning new styles. Even so, as renowned scholar Abraham Maslow has written, "many people assume that power in the form of strong leadership is always bad, overlooking the fact that there are healthy leaders whose motives are for the good of their organizations and for the good of society" (Goble, 2004: p. 97). So, which will it be -- authority-based leading or group-based leading? For decades, educators have appeared in limbo between the two, frustrating change and limiting reform.

The Not-So-Democratic Vote

As surreal as it seems, virtually all teachers already use a twin-poled model. However, the pole on the right is the democratic vote. Voting fails the participation test for three reasons. First, it favors students who are articulate, sometimes forceful, and can think on their feet. Second, the minority has ultimate control of the result. When at odds with voting's outcome, all they must do is nothing. A simple majority may carry the day, but implementing tight voting becomes a heartless activity with more than its share of gripes.

Third, there is the impact and concern; who is hit by this decision? And who might this decision hurt? These factors are often ignored when voting rises to the fore. After voting to keep their creative activities the same as the prior semester (reading, writing and journaling in 15-minute segments), teacher Kevin Hoonan (1996: p. 28) reaped disruption from two middle school boys. After collaborating with his class, the outcome was for students to set their own priorities during the hour. Moreover, his students decided the former division of labor was not even worth considering. This overturned their ballot! Only moments before, *repeating that course of action* had been the outcome of their vote.

Setting Teachers Free

Blending impact and concern into leading is a straightforward process for teachers who spell out their values. Where competing theories require leaders to change – consider Stephen Covey's *7 Habits of Highly Effective People* and Colin Powell's *13 Rules of Leadership* -- the Flex Leader or Bi-Polar model invites them to become more authentic within themselves. Positioning oneself along the chart begins the moment leaders examine their values.

Bi-Polar Leadership neither clarifies values nor raises skills. Rather, it provides a framework, a home for those tools. The result is color, vitality, flexibility, and a proactive dynamic – teachers choosing interventions, not feeling pushed and pulled by events. To reiterate, managing participatory management lets teachers become more of themselves, not less. Dr. Jon Kabat-Zinn, founder of the stress reduction clinic at the University of Massachusetts, writes, "It is impossible to become like somebody else. (To reduce stress) your only hope is to become more fully yourself" (Kabat-Zinn, J., 1990: p. 36).

Rewards

Flex Leader rewards go beyond internal harmony and personal growth. With the model in place, teachers increase student ownership in solutions, ease implementation, lift self-esteem, nourish *other* esteem, raise achievement, and disarm student bickering. With flex leading, teachers revitalize parent-support and soften the edge of administrators, governing agencies, and boards. Flex leading promises to brighten the classroom, stimulate creative thinking and prepare children for their uniquely interactive future.

A Critical Juncture in Education

Despite studies critical of schooling, educators remain respected in their community. Millions look to education, hungry for roles that bring citizens closer together and grown-ups closer to their kids. The public's objection to education reflects not so much a grievance as it does a forlorn hope.

Barbara Cervone, a former teacher and current president of What Kids Can Do, argues, "Never before in the history of U.S. Education has there been so much talk about school reform. Like the dieter who tries one plan after another, schools have remained largely impervious to attempts to change their shape" (Personal communication, 2014). Not a quick fix, converting to flex leading – polishing skills, training staff, orienting parents, coaching supervisory boards and community will take months, perhaps years. As a task force member of the Institute for Educational Leadership explains:

> "What we need is a partnership in which teachers are trained, encouraged, and required to be learners; where educators, legislators, and school board members are educated and informed about needs and issues, where everyone has a role to play, where there is no finger-pointing, where planning is collective, and where participants think outside the box together" (Task Force Member, Institute for Educational Leadership, 2001: p. 21).

Cervone continues, "A final element in good schools, often the ingredient that ties everything else together, is a collaborative approach to making decisions. . . . In schools that work, changes are not mandated, they are negotiated" (Personal communication, 2014). Collaboration can be the theme for the classroom, just as it can for the school environment. Yet, even children know collaboration cannot be the only method. Among the scores of decisions teachers make daily, only some are amenable to a form of negotiated settlement. The safety of children plus the weight of time combine to legitimize authority when such is the chosen path. The adventures of the 1990s taught us that while collaboration can be a choice, it cannot dominate the process. Time does not permit. A balance between authority and collaboration is required. This balance is where the Hersey/Blanchard model must finally bow to some form of group activity, leaving teachers with the ad hoc right to choose. Given, teachers can no longer control today's students. But they can control their flexible, Bi-Polar spectrum, a product of their own design.

Meanwhile, "We've managed to take the 15 years of children's lives that should be the most carefree, inquisitive, and memorable and fill them with a motley collection of stress and a neurotic fear of failure" (Gill, 2012). Yet nowhere is the need larger, the emotions greater, nor the investment higher than when a shift in grown-up thinking affects the future of our kids.

[Sidebar]

MEASURING TOOLS FOR BI-POLAR LEADING

Flexible leading corresponds to an index, as does the Hersey/Blanchard model. But for teachers locating themselves on the Hersey/Blanchard curve, this means using descriptors internal to the group. This confines H/B teachers to authority, even if authority is practiced *according to degree*. Twin-poled leaders, on the other hand, add measures that are external to their group. Such measures are then ranked according to individual preference. This gives flex teachers a personalized values system, a lens through which to view the selection of styles.

The resulting overlay then applies to choosing methods, not solutions. For solution finding, the values of the group come into play -- unless, of course, the teacher chooses authority. In that case, the teacher's values have control throughout, meaning of the process and of the solution as well.

Below, the left column ranks my own values when I began The Collaborative Center in 1985. Thirty years with tinkering has meant personal growth and change, (a point about which my friends occasionally agree). Today, employees and students are more likely to know me by the schedule on the right. Although as a reader, you might wonder why I chose these values, or ranked them as I did, that type of exercise is irrelevant. Subordinates don't need to comprehend your reasoning. They need to see what you believe in and to observe you being consistent, especially as you flex among styles. Your standards and your *consistency* will become clear. They mark you as their leader.

The Author-as-Leader

VALUES (1985)		VALUES (Today)	
Policy		Safety	High
Safety		Impact	
Time		Concern	
Control (my need for)		Trust	W
Knowledge		Flexibility	E
Trust	⇐ Hersey/	Knowledge	I
Closeness	Blanchard ⇒	Closeness	G
Impact		Mood	H
Concern		Priorities	T
Mood (mine)		Policy	
Priorities		Time	
Flexibility		Control	Low

(Source: Author)

Think about what is important to you as you position yourself along the chart. For example, if you generally want accountability, you probably lean toward the left. If you prefer involvement, you tend toward the right. The job of teasing these general terms into detailed descriptors falls to each teacher. Look under the surface of the words. Does "involvement" mean connecting, bonding, fresh ideas, sharing responsibility, a sounding board? When you can list what you believe are the benefits of involvement, you will be looking in the direction of your values.

Even in bad light, insight into these values is not as timorous as I have made it appear. For example, although listing "keeping my job" might feel humbling, it is supported by enough awareness to make Abraham Maslow proud, certainly in the current economy. Be honest about what drives you. Acknowledging one's tendencies is crucial to effective leadership. It helps students understand your leading and gets you thinking about your chart.

When it comes to influencing others, only phony participators (phony collaborators, manipulators and phony consulters) have more trouble than the pure authoritarian. If you are not an authoritarian, yet find that resistance is robbing you of confidence, it may be that you need to behave more intuitively and get proactive about this chart. The sense that the Bi-Polar Menu is leading you may simply mean you are not leading it.

Chapter 5

MILLENIAL CHILDREN AND NO CHILD LEFT BEHIND

"A child miseducated is a child lost."

John F. Kennedy

The decade long thrust toward standardized testing has been a tragic error. In districts where children cannot compete, dropout rates still soar. States, realizing the cost of testing, are waiving and even reversing the requirements of No Child Left Behind (NCLB). State after state demands relief from its draconian demands. In Maryland, Montgomery County School Superintendent Joshua Starr rejects NCLB Funding, citing his district's own nationally recognized evaluation system. He calls for a three-year moratorium on standardized tests. (Strauss, 2012). Idaho, Montana and South Dakota threaten to ignore the law altogether (McNeil, 2011). Testifying before congress, New York City teacher Jia Lee calls NCLB a "great crime" (Lee, 2015). Seattle Education Association President Jonathan Knapp categorically states "Almost everything about No Child Left Behind is wrong" (Personal conversation, November 5, 2016).

It is not the tests as such that disturb kids. Teens say the tests are challenging; they are a rush. It is the myopic focus on preparation that troubles educators and children alike. In the classroom, the pressure on teacher and child is intense. Berkeley professor David Kirp calls schools a "pressure cooker,' and states "students have become test-taking robots, sitting through as many as 20 standardized tests a year" (Kirp, 2015, para 5).

Everyone -- teachers, parents, administrators, citizens, students -- wants children to be evaluated. But we want them to grow emotionally and socially as well, in other words equally during their hours in school. In the 1960s Abraham Maslow decried "education which concerns itself with grades, credits and diplomas rather than wisdom, understanding and good judgment" (Hoffman, E., 1988, p. 104).

More recently, educator Mary Futrell writes, "The standards movement and the requirements of No Child Left Behind made it abundantly clear: we can't simply set goals and then punish people for not achieving them." (Rubin, H., 2009, p. xi) As an increasing number of parents opt their children out of standardized tests, they do so for many reasons, "including the stress they believe it brings on young students, discomfort with tests being used to gauge teacher performance, fear that corporate influence is overriding education and concern that test prep is narrowing curricula down to the minimum needed to pass an exam" (Zezima, 2013, para. 2). Merrimack College Dean of Education, Dan Butin adds, ". . . assessments can never tell the full story of a child" (Butin, D., 2012).

Finally, Congress is tackling the uproar created by its own law. Kentucky Senator Rand Paul "wants to repeal the law and says many students have been failed by the current system" (n/a, Town News Online, January 29, 2015). Senator Patty Murray, the ranking Democrat on the Senate's Education Committee, writes, "NCLB has proved to be a deeply broken law with unrealistic requirements. It is hindering [teachers'] efforts and needs to be fixed" (Murray, 2015).

WHAT'S AT STAKE WITH HIGH STAKES TESTS

Here is the problem. The push toward standardized tests is more than a way to measure individual progress. It is also a way to hand out pass/fail grades to schools, thereby holding teachers accountable, but in only a single dimension, content. As 2012 National Superintendent of the Year, Heath Morrison asks, "Why are we in a rush to do all this testing, then use it for accountability for schools and for accountability for teachers?" Morrison calls testing "an egregious waste of taxpayer dollars that won't help kids." (The Charlotte Observer online, Dec. 27, 2012, para. 12).

So long as emotional and social growth are excluded from the equation, three things are wrong with this approach. First, the grades handed to schools are a false litmus test for progress; damage is not being measured. While in cross-section, the 2015 drop-out rate is low, the United States high school *graduation* rate ranks in the bottom fourth of developed nations (OECD, 2014). This is because in lower income communities – home to so-called drop-out factories -- less than half the freshman class will graduate on time. (Koebler, 2011, para 1). Children from these locales are the poor and minority children George Bush's education law was designed to assist (Hefling, 2015). Yet more than eight thousand students leave formal schooling daily, most from impoverished communities (StatisticBrain.org, 2014). So much for No Child Left Behind. Education creates waves of youth left behind like the Tune In, Turn On, Drop Out druggie generation of the 1960s. Poor and minority youngsters are voting with their feet.

Second, education proceeds not just in math and reading, but also in breadth and depth. In the early days of the Bush administration, Washington State's Commission on Student Learning met to hammer out standards for No Child Left Behind. I attended those meetings as an observer. Although commission members included district superintendents, most came from Corporate America. Fredrick Taylor, the father of time-and-motion studies – Taylor introduced force-feeding to industrial production in 1881 – could not have been more pleased. Taylor's effort was to standardize the nation's workforce by timing factory workers on their every move. Although scientific management (Taylorism) as a distinct theory was obsolete by the 1930s, *most of its themes are still important parts of industrial management today* (ibiblio.org., 2013, para. 2). The problem is, teachers are not industrialists. They want teaching to be about creativity, civics, and emotional development. They know and understand the in-depth growing that must take place in their charges. They are the professionals. They can be trusted to know schooling's larger purpose whereas corporate executives cannot.

Standardization is not the answer. Frederick Taylor is simply another hawk for content. As educator and author Dr. Rubin writes,

> "Despite the fact that today, most schools continue to prepare young learners to be storage banks of knowledge and skills that they can

summon on demand and exhibit on high stakes tests, we know that this type of accountability captures only a small portion of what we need from public education – and what today's and tomorrow's learners will need to succeed." (Rubin, H., 2009, p. 26). Teacher and author Jesse Hagopian adds, "I'm opposed to these tests because they narrow what education is supposed to be about and they lower kids' horizons. I think collaboration, imagination, critical thinking skills are all left off these tests and can't be assessed by circling in A, B, C or D" (Zezima, 2013, para. 6)

Finally, there is the military axiom that leaders dare not issue directives that cannot be enforced. The loss of influence and respect are simply too great.

At Seattle's Garfield High School, January 9, 2013 was examination day. No kids showed up to be tested. The reason? No tests were set. Garfield teachers had earlier boycotted the exam, refusing to administer it. Saying the MAP test (Measure of Academic Progress) was flawed and students were sabotaging the outcomes because they knew the results made no difference in their grade, Garfield's staff unanimously determined to defy their district. There is no greater disrespect for leadership than to flout the leader's dictates. And there is no greater trepidation on the part of leaders than a mandate of their own would reap an act of mutiny, of absolute disobedience.

Parents have also taken up the cudgel, willingly joining the acrimony over accountability. In Compton,

California, hundreds of parent-protesters marched on Los Angeles education headquarters demanding a charter takeover of their neighborhood school. The Parent Revolution, which championed the McKinley School march under California's Parent Empowerment Act of 2010, heralded the action as if the French had again stormed the Bastille. The group called December 8, 2010, an historic day (McDonald, 2010). True, some 200 schools (of 800) in the Los Angeles District had failed to meet No Child Left Behind standards (Op/Ed Seattle Times online, Dec. 28, 2012), and as Parent Revolution chief Benjamin Austin says, apart from his revolution, "There is no consequence for failure and no reward for success" (Austin, 2012).

So, Austin would add another layer to the demand for accountability. In a demonstration of futility, California's so-called *trigger law*, which granted take-over power to parents, was watered "almost beyond recognition" by Julia Brownley, the state's Education Committee chairwoman (Austin, 2009). This weakening of the trigger law took place after Brownley entertained dozens of parents testifying about the importance of parent influence in their local schools. Brownley's version of the new law meant failing schools would foster nothing more than a "meaningless and patronizing hearing" (Austin, 2009). The chairwoman announced her version with "great fanfare, *saying she had heard the call of the parents*" (Austin, 2009). In fact, Brownley flinched. She placed herself as a phony consulter, that high-risk position, top left on the twin polar chart. Outraged by Brownley's stance, McKinley's parents marched.

DECIDING HOW TO DECIDE?

Arguably, a charter operator for McKinley Elementary might work as the parents anticipate. (The issue is mute. A legal technicality caused the parent's petition to be thrown out). However, the outcome is not what matters here. It is *the way things get decided* that puts McKinley children at risk. Reports of threatened retribution and even physical provocation dot the debate. (Wilson, 2011, pg.1) Even the name *revolution* seems overpowering. Inflamed rhetoric does nothing to further a good-faith caucus between educators, parents, the larger community, and certainly students themselves.

The McKinley charter has proven to be a non-starter. But to carry on the debate in spiteful terms sets a dangerous precedent for McKinley's kids. They will learn about political power soon enough. They need a more creative solution now, while they are still innocent and can profit from a more collegial approach. Here, again is Dr. Rubin;

> "The message of [my] book, COLLABORATIVE LEADERSHIP, is families, communities, educators, business leaders and policy makers are engaged in an ongoing relationship and share responsibility for the education of our children and youth. This teamwork ... deserves much more attention if we want to improve our schools and other public agencies to insure our children's future" (Rubin, 2009, p. 42).

NEW STANDARDS FOR A NEW AGE

Rubin's *ongoing relationship* would mean parties would have to abandon the Industrial Era anthem in which competition, not cooperation guides the debate. Today's students are not growing up in the Industrial Age. They were not even born in it. A list of desired characteristics of workers during the Industrial Era comes from Irving Burstiner. It was published near the end of that era, in 1984. In his classic, but dated lament, Burstiner called for a revival of the values shown below.

- Good level of productivity
- Consistency
- Honesty
- Loyalty to the firm
- No rocking the boat
- Pleasant personality
- Promptness
- Proper behavior on the job
- Regular attendance and
- Respect for authority

What if attributes of today's worker could connect with Burstiner's tenets while simultaneously replacing those values? For each of the 1984 bullets, a behavior characteristic of the Age of Information can be substituted. Keep in mind that today, no one person has enough information to make decisions in solitude, even in consultation, *which still smacks of isolation.*

For good level of productivity, one can name good level of *creativity*. For consistency, *contribution;*

for honesty, *disclosure*; for loyalty to the firm, loyalty to the *process*; for pleasant personality, *effective* personality; for no rocking the boat, *rocking* the boat; for promptness, *results*; for proper behavior, *innovative* behavior; for respect for authority, respect for *ideas*; and for regular attendance, *total* attendance.

Whatever Burstiner's intention, his characteristics no longer fit today's workplace, certainly not the classroom. In fact, so long as content and accountability remain pivotal to school reform, corporate philanthropies such as the Gates and Broad Foundations will aggregate power, districts will continue to circle the wagons, young people will continue to drop out, parents will continue to receive carefully vetted information, teachers will continue their frustration and principals will continue to hold tight to the reins. No one can fault the administrator who says, *If my ship is going down, I will be the man at the helm.* Yet together, these factors stifle collaboration, create winners and losers, and perpetuate the competitive mentality of an outmoded age.

THE PHENOMENON OF BELONGING

If one word could summarize the difference between the Industrial Age and the Age of Information, that word would be belonging. As it stands today, education is a closed community. It is closed to parents and it is closed to children. There is significant debate whether it exists for children *at all*. Austin's League of Education Voters believes it exists for adults. Michelle Rhee, the ousted chancellor of District of Columbia schools, echoes the league's position. Rhee states,

"Policy makers, district administrators, and school boards... have created a bureaucracy that is focused on the adults instead of students" (Rhee, 2010, p. 41). Except for a supporting role, belonging to the school community is rarely an option for children and families.

In one small Caribbean country, airport visitors are greeted with two large signs: BELONGERS and VISITORS. As Pew Foundation Director Suzanne Morse writes, "The volumes written today about leadership fail to recognize the motivation and the necessity of belonging in leadership preparation and selection. The heart of leadership, 'belonging to a community and its common interest is lost.' All learning... is rooted in the human need to feel a sense of belonging and contributing to a community" Morse, S. (2009), p.17).

In our culture, there is evidence that children are positioned for belonging more than is commonly known. Why are they being denied? Once again, Maslow's hierarchy is revealing. Maslow distinguished between basic needs and what he called Meta, or growth needs. In cross section, basic needs have been provided through the prosperity of the Industrial Era. Still for students to grow socially and emotionally, they must feel they belong. Among the needs that (normally) are met prior to belonging, Maslow included self-esteem. (Anyone who thinks children's esteem is not vital to a school culture should try mocking a child in the classroom. Action from the ACLU will not be far behind!)

For three decades, the theme of self-esteem has been pivotal to the school curriculum, creating a disconnect when it comes to incorporating a child's voice in decision-making. Children are prepared to assume a greater sense of belonging. In fact, they go to great lengths to belong – they simply do not include adults in their community. (See Maslow's Needs Box above)

In a collaborative environment, belonging becomes real. In Coeur d'Alene, Idaho, teacher Melita Clary collaborated with her kids over semester rules. "Actually, I didn't need to give anything beyond my need for order," she writes. "If any idea went against my need, the rest of the children spoke out against it."

For Clary's new students, cooperation was not the norm. Clary's class came with a reputation for trouble. After they collaborated, one girl came to her in tears, "You're the first teacher that gave our class a chance." Teachers collaborating with their students, parents collaborating with teachers -- parents will not march in protest on a collaborative school; their children will not allow it.

In fact, it is children who will remind us to collaborate. Author/therapist Charlotte Kasl describes a stalemate when her 14-year-old daughter wanted to see a movie and mother was too sick to drive her. After examining needs, they reached a solution together. When Kasl next faced a row with her daughter, the youngster pleaded, "Can it be like the time at the movies? Tell me the two sides" (Kasl, C., 1989, p. 271).

Clary, too, sometimes overlooks the chance to collaborate. She writes, "You can be sure the kids will remind me." Tom Gordon's own children have been known to force the issue. Once when Gordon was about to pronounce a decision, his daughter held up an index finger and mouthed, Method One, the win-lose method described earlier. Gordon quickly backtracked and asked for his daughter's needs.

Junior high school teacher Gloria Tyler says, "When students partner with their teacher and are allowed to join in the decision-making process, they begin to 'own' part of the classroom system. In that ownership, they become less disruptive, instead more relaxed and engaged learners" (Tyler, 2015, personal communication).

THE INADEQUACY OF AUTHORITY

Why would teachers not look for alternatives to authority? Look at the factors that are leveraging here; first, just as in education, the corporate world is dramatically linked. No single person has all the answers. Bosses that rely exclusively on the hierarchy of their position are routinely referred to as Type A or micro managers. To avoid the stigma, they hold meetings. Meetings that disregard the voices of subordinates lose the feedback managers deeply need. Meetings that take place simply to announce a decision are a disaster. This is no more so than when the convener has positioned herself as having heard their peoples' concerns. As California's Julia Brownley learned, those only result in hostility and resentment.

Children need to prepare for a highly interconnected world. They need teachers who can listen and can spark creativity; when it comes to classroom decision-making, they need a genuine airing of ideas. And why not? Famed researcher Rensis Likert once noted that when managers allow participation, the men at the top actually have more influence rather than less. "That is, in a team environment, the more power you give to someone else, the more you have for yourself" (Goble, 2005, p. 20).

Second, there is the business of social media. Most of our young people use Facebook and texting to exchange ideas with contemporaries across the country and even globe. The phenomenon has been the topic of much study, and its bonding element among young people has been described. Our children are simply accustomed to connecting, uniting on a genuinely intimate level. They need the same from their schooling. (We should not overlook that in many cases, they get a degree of intimacy, of togetherness from their social media. The tipping point remains distant before children enjoy similar fruits from collaborative deciding.)

Third, the Industrial Hierarchy has collapsed. Apart from military and paramilitary organizations, Command-and-Control has done nothing to redeem itself since Harvard's Rosabeth Moss Kanter wrote that the hierarchy would collapse of its own weight. Kanter likened global economic competition to the Olympics. The winners in *these* games would be non-hierarchical, co-operative, focused on process—the way things are done. They would also, she said, have a dose of humility. (Kanter, 1989). The flattening of the hierarchy that took place in the '90s was designed to create a more streamlined organization. It did that. But it also riffed mid-level managers and doubled the workload of those who stayed behind. Today, there are even books about Bottom Up Leadership, for example, *How to Manage Your Manager*, and *Followership: How Followers Are Creating Change and Changing Leaders*. Understandably, Top-Down management has lost much of its fabled cache.

Fourth, there is the Bart Simpson Effect – our kids believe they can say anything that comes to mind. Thanks to many years of applied psychology in our nation's schools, children have become remarkably in touch with their inner musings -- and eager to let everyone know what those are. The result is children who are more than outspoken; they believe their every notion *must* be aired. No wonder they clamor for collaboration once they have tried it out.

Fifth is the business of self-esteem. Unlike most adults, kids were not raised in a culture of sin, guilt and redemption (Leins, C., 2015). They do not comprehend it. Their esteem will not allow. A function of applied psychology that has informed teaching for the past thirty years, the esteem movement will never reverse itself. It is here to impact us, well, forever. What that means is children not only gushing with ideas, but also seeing their ideas as necessary to the outcome of an event.

Finally, there is the Information Age. The Age of Industry has passed, leaving a legacy of triumph and domination that now is being eroded by a global economy, one that sees goods produced abroad. The U.S. economy, on the other hand, is based on service, service that involves the sharing of information. This may seem trite; most know about this quantum shift already. Still it is a factor because today's youth knows nothing of the heyday of industrial life. They know little, of the exponential growth that marked the economic wave following World War Two. They only know about their laptops, their tablets, their iPhones, and the information to be found there, all of which is shared. However we misconstrue it, connecting is their world.

Taken together, corporate connectivity, social networking, the demise of the hierarchy, children's verbosity, the self-esteem movement, and the reality of the Information Age all point to collaboration as the way out of education's abyss. While the above items might seem enigmatic, a problem to some, they can also be looked at as the ingredients for a collaborative school culture. Yes, taken separately they might seem problematic. Taken together, they might simply describe the detritus of the Industrial Era, and the Top Down model which it brought to bear.

GIVING PARTICIPATION ANOTHER CHANCE

Today we are at a crossroads. The Human Potential Movement of the 1990's failed. It failed because of resistance to viewing the human as our greatest underdeveloped strength. The Human Being remains an untapped asset. But what does that mean in the face of how teachers teach? It means little more than an invitation, a plea for a second chance. Collaborative endeavor stands like the proverbial low-hanging fruit. The main ingredients are present – the attending skills of teachers and the exuberance of kids – and the cost is nothing save a few minutes away from test prep and standardized content. All that is needed is the support of administrators and parents. . . and patience on the part of the Corporate Agenda.

Summary

Education's cast of characters has changed. Once teachers were the workers, principals the managers, children the raw material (and eventual product), and the consumer was business and industry. In today's world, the division of labor is far more complex. Children and teachers together are the workers. Curriculum, books and experience are the raw materials. Kids' creativity and ideas are the product, and the consumer is an entire society.

Most important, education's investors were formerly the society at large. Now students do the investing. And many of today's youth are withdrawing their equity. Rather than face a classroom where they feel they do not belong, they are opting for low paying jobs and the tedious task of living at home. They are simply not willing to be judged on their ability to stockpile knowledge and vomit it up on high-stakes tests. If that's all education is about, they are willing to risk a future life on the streets.

It is said that teachers make hundreds of decisions every day, striving to solve classroom problems that occupy part of each day's labor. Children are prepared to take part in those outcomes, at least on occasion and to an extent. They are being blocked by time-intensive test prep and the teacher's vestiges interest in command-and-control. Collaborative leadership offers a path which educators can follow to bring out the healthy values of today's kids, can give them a sense of belonging to something greater than themselves. It can provide the social bonding that keeps children enthusiastic and keeps our youth in school.

EPILOGUE

"Because relationships are at the core of collaboration, an easy case can be made that the most important public context for doing collaboration is in and around our public schools"

Hank Rubin

One might argue that the most important public context for collaboration is in Washington D.C. But let's get real. Adversarial politics gets in the way. Michigan Representative Justin Amash states, "Our politics is in a partisan death spiral" as he abandons the GOP in 2019. Still it is notable that Congress, as of December 2015, has shown uncommon unanimity in returning No Child Left Behind to the states. It will be interesting to see if such bi-partisanship will last. It bears pointing out that our children's education will likely remain in state oversight. The Federal Government is finished with micro-managing education. *That* will certainly last. Its interference with our children was based on Texas' unproven model; for 15 years the boondoggle has left a legacy of negativity toward our schools – both on the part of adults and children alike. No one dare ask if school violence is a product of overwhelm, hostility, and resentment; a culture of punitive indifference.

On December 10th, 2015, President Obama announced the failure of No Child Left Behind together with the demise of his own Race to the

Top. According to the laws of scientific experiment, failure does represent an advance. That is because a trial doesn't have to be repeated. But here the Law of Unintended Consequences must include a generation of kids struggling to understand. That they are so adept, so enamored with the collaborative method must leave them wondering what happened to their formative years. From athletes to musicians to husbands and wives, no one ever achieved when external pressures forced them to perform beyond what they could comprehend.

Say this for No Child Left Behind – testing is good. It gives us a yardstick to measure individual progress as well as a comparison with students abroad. Children expect to be tested. Teachers expect to be evaluated. But no test has ever measured head-in-the-game -- giving 100% effort -- as well as individual teachers, who are schooled in doing exactly that. It is the uber testing, the myopic focus on excessive tests to both gauge student progress and evaluate teacher effectiveness, that frustrated lawmakers, administrators, staff and students alike.

With education having been repossessed by the states, it is an interesting time to try something new. This time cannot be a repeat of "decentralized" deciding of the '90s. Unguided caucuses, whether at the classroom or school level, only result in time consuming bitch sessions.

This time let's make it a genuine experiment, not one with a foregone conclusion, say *"100 percent of students will perform at grade level"* as the 2002 law decreed (NCLB). If states are truly committed to "replacing some drill-and-kill memorization with hands-on learning and critical thinking" (Kirp, 2015), then collaborative deciding, beginning by equating the needs of student and teacher, would seem an enticing place to begin. Switching to a collaborative climate in place of command-and-control will require courage on the part of principal and staff. But the resulting school culture promises to be a place of vitality and excitement rather than fear and submission. As that happens, we will all be glad to "consign No Child Left Behind to the dustbin of history" (Kirp, 2015, para 1).

REFERENCES

Amash, Justin, July 4, 2019, Washington Post Op-Ed, "Our politics is trapped in a partisan death spiral."

Anderson, P., (1990), *Great Quotes from Great Leaders*, Successories Publishing, Lombard, IL.

Armario, C. 2011. "Other States Joining Idaho in Defying No Child Left Behind." *Seattle Times*, July 21

Austin, B., (2009), Put Power Over California's Schools in Hands of Parents, *Los Angeles Times, Online, OP/Ed.* http://articles.latimes.com/2009/dec/16/opinion/la-oe-austin16-2009dec16

Austin, B., (2012), Address at Aki Kurose Middle School, Seattle, WA.

Butin, D., *Arm teachers! A response to the NRA. HuffPost,* Dec. 21, 2012 http://www.huffingtonpost.com/dan-w-butin/arm-teachers-a-response-t_b_2349845.htmlCharlotte Observer, (2012), Anothersuperintendentcomesoutagainsttesting, https://educationclearinghouse.wordpress.com/2012/12/27/another-superintendent-comes-out-against-testing/

Covey, S. 1989. *The 7 Habits of Highly Effective People.* Kindle Edition.

Daft, R.L. (2013), *Organizational Theory and Design*, 11th Ed. Mason, OH: Cengage Learning.

Eldritch Press. 2013. "Frederick Winslow Taylor"" ibiblio.org

Elliott, P., (2013), Youth unemployment: 15 percent of American youth out of school and Work, *Huffington Post online.* http://www.

huffingtonpost.com/2013/10/21/youth-unemployment_n_4134358.html

Fisher and Ury (1981), *Getting to Yes; Negotiating Agreement Without Giving In*, Houghton Mifflin Company, Boston/New York leadership/

Gill, A. A. (2012). Schools are Ruining our Kids, *Vanity Fair Online*, Dec. 2012. Retrieved from http://www.vanityfair.com/society/2012/12/aa-gill-schools-ruining-our-kids.

Goble, F. (2004). *The Third Force*. Chapel Hill, NC: Maurice Bassett Publishing.

Gordon, T. (1977). *Leader Effectiveness Training* (1st ed.). New York, NY: Wyden Books.

Gordon, T., (1974) *Teacher effectiveness training*, New York, McKay Books

Greenleaf, R., (2015), What is Servant Leadership? https://greenleaf.org/what-is-servant-leadership

Hefling, K., (2015), Too Much Testing in Schools? Senate Panel Considers Changes, Associated Press, January 21st.

Heider, J. (1986). *The Tao of Leadership*, Kindle edition

Helms, K., 2015. "New State Tests Waste Tax Dollars." *Charlotte Observer*, December 27th.

Hersey, P. (1984). *The Situational Leader*. New York, NY: Warner Books.

Hoffman, E., (1988), Maslow: The Right to be Human, New York, *Tarcher/Penguin books*.

Hoonan, K. (1996). Collaborating with the Middle School Classroom. *The Emergency Librarian, 23* (3). (Now *The Teacher Librarian*) ibiblio.org., para. 2 http://www.ibiblio.org/eldritch/fwt/taylor.html

Institute for Educational Leadership. (2001, April). Redefining the Teacher as Leader. *Schools for the 21st Century Annual Report*, 21.

Josephson, M. and Moyers, B. (1988). A world of ideas. *PBS TV.*

Kabat-Zinn, J. (1990). *Full Catastrophe Living.* New York, NY: Delacorte Press.

Kanter, R. M., (1990), When giants learn to dance, New York, *Routledge publishers.*

Kasl, C., (1989), Women, sex, and addiction; A search for love and power, New York, *Harper & Row, publishers.*

Kellerman, B., (2008), Followership: How Followers are Creating Change and Changing Leaders, Harvard University Press, Boston, MA

Kellerman, B., (2010), Leadership: Essential Selections on Power, Authority, and Influence, McGraw Hill, New York, N.Y.

Kellerman, B., (2012), The End of Leadership, Harper Collins, New York, N.Y.

Kirp, d., (2015), Left behind no longer, Why the new education law is good for children left behind, *New York Times*, Dec. 10, 2015, http://www.nytimes.com/2015/12/10/opinion/why-the-new-education-law-is-good-for-children-left-behind.html? ref=topics

Koebler, J., (2011), How to identify a high school dropout factory, *U.S. News, Education* http://www.usnews.com/education/blogs/high-school-notes/2011/11/30/how-to-identify-a-high-school-dropout-factory

Lee, Jia, (2015), Senate hearings reauthorization of NCLB, *nLightn Media* http://vimeo.com/117989096?can_id=&source=email-endannualtesting-only-two-days-left-to-join-npes-letter-writing-campaign-to-congress.

Leins, C., (2015), Americans Becoming Less Religious Thanks to Millennials, U.S. News and World Report, November 3, http://www.msn.com/en-us/news/us/americans-becoming-less-religious-thanks-to-millennials/ar-BBmNSus?li=BBgzzfc&ocid=U146DHP

McDonald, P.R., (2010), Compton parents petition to take over chronically failing public school through 'Parent Trigger' law, send shock waves throughout the nation, *Los Angeles News, The Informer*, Dec. 8, 2010. http://www.laweekly.com/news/compton-parents-petition-to-take-over-chronically-failing-public-school-through-parent-trigger-law-send-shock-waves-throughout-the-nation-2393224

McNeil, M., (2011), More states defiant on NCLB compliance,*Education Week Spotlight*,http://www.edweek.org/ew/articles/2011/07/06/36nclb.h30.html

McNeil, M. 2011. "More States Defiant on NCLB Compliance." Education Week Spotlight.

MacGregor, D., (2015), The Problem with Theory X, http://www.envisionsoftware.com/articles/Theory_X.html

Maslow, A., (2015), http://www.envisionsoftware.com/articles/Maslows_Needs_Hierarchy.html

MetLife Foundation. (2010). Survey of the American Teacher. Retrieved on July 27, 2013 from: http://www.metlife.com/about/corporate-profile/citizenship/metlife-foundation/metlife-survey-of-the-american-teacher.html?WT.mc_id=vu1101

Mill, J.S., 185. On Liberty. Retrieved from hfund. orttp://oll.libertyg, Quote 201

Milner, M. 2015. *Freaks, Geeks, and Cool Kids.* Routledge

Morse, S., (2009), New metaphors for leadership, *Civic Partners, Annual report of the Pew Foundation.*

Murray, Sen. P., (2015), Congress needs to fix outdated federal No Child Left Behind education law, *Op/Ed, The Seattle Times*, January 22, 2015.

OECD, (2014), Organization for Economic Cooperation and Development. http://www.aneki.com/oecd_countries_high_school_graduation_rates.html?number=25

Piercey, D., (2010), Why don't teachers collaborate? Kappan Magazine, Plato, (380 BCE), The Republic,

Rhee, M., (2010), What I've learned, *Newsweek*, Dec. 13, 2010, Vol. 156, Issue, 24.

Rubin, H., (2009), Collaborative leadership, *Corwin/Sage*, Thousand Oaks, CA.

Statistic Brain, (2014), http://www.statisticbrain.com/high-school-dropout-statistics/

Strauss, V., (2012), Montgomery County schools chief calls for three-year moratorium on standardized testing, *Washington Post*, Washington, D.C. http://www.washingtonpost.com/blogs/answer-sheet/wp/2012/12/10/moco-schools-chief-calls-for-three-year-moratorium-on-standardized-testing/

Thatcher, M. Consensus Is the Absence of Leadership. Retrieved on Jan 30, 2014 from: *Http://www.mjldomain.com/Opinions/Opinions/***leadership***.*

Trump, D. 1987, The Art of the Deal. New York, N.Y. Random House.

Wilson, S., Pulling the trigger on failing schools, *LA Weekly*, Dec. 1, 2011. http://www.laweekly.com/

news/pulling-the-trigger-on-failing-schools-2173138

Woodbury, S., (2014), para. 3. http://www.sarahwoodbury.com/life-expectancy-in-the-middle-ages/

Zezima, K., (2013), More parents opting kids out of standardized tests, *Huffington Post, Parents,* http://www.huffingtonpost.com/2013/09/09/opt-out-standardized-tests_n_3893885.html

Zuckert, C. 2014. "Machiavelli and the End of Nobility in Politics." Social Research: An International Quarterly 81. no. 1 (Spring, 2014). http://muse.jhu.edu/article/543793/pdf

APPENDIX 1

FACILITATION FLOW CHART

SET-UP: Identify the Facilitator and the Concern

NEEDS OF A

NEEDS OF B

STEPS AND THE "UMBRELLA" WORD (or Phrase)

(1) How Can We _____ So That _____

(2) SOLUTIONS

(3) Evaluate

(4)

(5) IMPLEMENTATION

Solution

(6) FOLLOW-UP

Reproducible: for teachers to track their own collaborations as they move along.

APPENDIX 2

AUTHORITY BASE

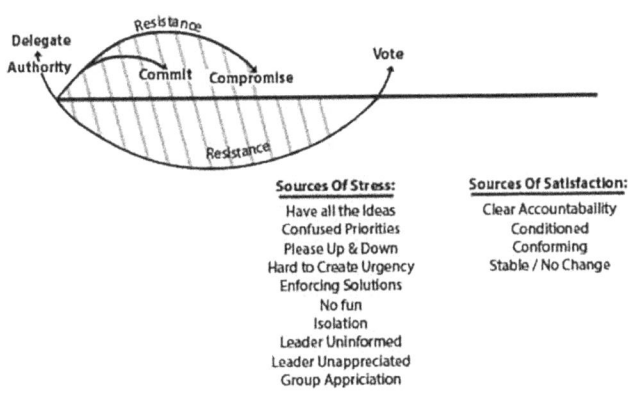

Teachers using the bi-polar design will find themselves with two or three to as many as a half-dozen preferred interventions, seldom more. This diagram lists the advantages and limitations of those whose preferred base is in authority. The term 'base' simply means the option of first refusal – nothing is negotiable except issues which demand to be negotiated. Authority-based teachers should expect resistance to direct them to alternative styles, as indicated above.

APPENDIX 3

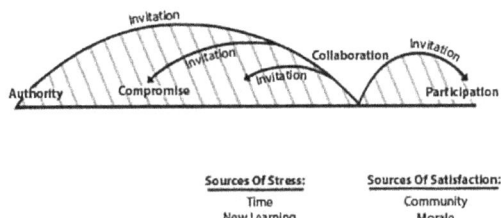

COLLABORATION BASE

© Center for Collaboration and Teamwork
12/89 (Revised January 1993)

For teachers based in collaboration, all things are negotiable except those which prove otherwise. Here, the teacher/leader will be coaxed by invitation to the more suitable style. Regardless of which pole the teacher chooses as a base, he/she does not give up the neutral position atop the chart.

Tom Gordon once said, leaders spend 20 percent of their time solving problems, another 20 percent of the time there are no problems. The remaining 60 percent of the time leaders go around solving problems that do not exist. Imagine teachers having 80 percent of their time available for teaching.

ABOUT THE AUTHOR

Don Broadwell began studying collaborative leadership in 1982 after a career counselor advised him to shed the top-down style he learned in the Marines. Following seven years in the military and in grad school, Don spent a career in sales, supplying library books to schools. He retired after 40 years, but continues to train teachers on nights and weekends, as he has for the past three decades.

    Don's CV includes an undergraduate degree in mathematics and a Princeton Theological Seminary degree in counseling. Don has taught collaborative leadership for the University of Idaho (Coeur d'Alene), for Seattle Pacific University, and for Green River College (Seattle). He directs the Collaborative Center in suburban Maple Valley. His breakout workshops for national audiences include the Association of Experiential Education and the Association of Federally Employed Women. Don can be reached at donbroadwell@the-collaborative-center.org or by contacting the publisher.

www.ingramcontent.com/pod-product-compliance
Ingram Content Group UK Ltd.
Pitfield, Milton Keynes, MK11 3LW, UK
UKHW022215230426
12048UKWH00016BA/856